T0060721

How to Write a Marketing Plan

CREATING SUCCESS
SERIES

Dealing with Difficult People Roy Lilley

Decision Making and Problem Solving John Adair

Develop Your Leadership Skills John Adair

Develop Your Presentation Skills Theo Theobald

How to Manage People Michael Armstrong

How to Manage Projects Paul J Fielding

How to Organize Yourself John Caunt

How to Work Remotely Gemma Dale

How to Write a Business Plan Brian Finch

How to Write a Marketing Plan John Westwood

How to Write Reports and Proposals Patrick Forsyth

Improve Your Communication Skills Alan Barker

Successful Time Management Patrick Forsyth

The above titles are available from all good bookshops.

For further information on these and other Kogan Page titles, or to order online, visit www.koganpage.com.

Seventh edition

How to Write a Marketing Plan

Define your strategy,
plan effectively and reach
your marketing goals

John Westwood

KoganPage

Publisher's note
Every possible effort has been made to ensure that the information contained in this book is accurate at the time of going to press, and the publishers and authors cannot accept responsibility for any errors or omissions, however caused. No responsibility for loss or damage occasioned to any person acting, or refraining from action, as a result of the material in this publication can be accepted by the editor, the publisher or the author.

First published in Great Britain and the United States in 1996 by Kogan Page Limited
Seventh edition 2022

Apart from any fair dealing for the purposes of research or private study, or criticism or review, as permitted under the Copyright, Designs and Patents Act 1988, this publication may only be reproduced, stored or transmitted, in any form or by any means, with the prior permission in writing of the publishers, or in the case of reprographic reproduction in accordance with the terms and licences issued by the CLA. Enquiries concerning reproduction outside these terms should be sent to the publishers at the undermentioned addresses:

2nd Floor, 45 Gee Street	8 W 38th Street, Suite 902	4737/23 Ansari Road
London	New York, NY 10018	Daryaganj
EC1V 3RS	USA	New Delhi 110002
United Kingdom		India
www.koganpage.com		

© John Westwood, 1996, 2000, 2006, 2013, 2016, 2019, 2022

The right of John Westwood to be identified as the author of this work has been asserted by him in accordance with the Copyright, Designs and Patents Act 1988.

ISBNs
Hardback   978 1 3986 0570 1
Paperback   978 1 3986 0568 8
Ebook   978 1 3986 0569 5

British Library Cataloguing-in-Publication Data

A CIP record for this book is available from the British Library.

Library of Congress Cataloging-in-Publication Data
Names: Westwood, John, 1947- author.
Title: How to write a marketing plan: define your strategy, plan
    effectively and reach your marketing goals / John Westwood.
Description: Seventh edition. | London, United Kingdom; New York, NY:
    Kogan Page, 2022. | Series: Creating success series
Identifiers: LCCN 2022008071 (print) | LCCN 2022008072 (ebook) | ISBN
    9781398605688 (paperback) | ISBN 9781398605701 (hardback) | ISBN
    9781398605695 (ebook)
Subjects: LCSH: Marketing–Management.
Classification: LCC HF5415.13 .W48 2022 (print) | LCC HF5415.13 (ebook) |
    DDC 658.8/02–dc23/eng/20220222
LC record available at https://lccn.loc.gov/2022008071
LC ebook record available at https://lccn.loc.gov/2022008072

Typeset by Hong Kong FIVE Workshop
Print production managed by Jellyfish
Printed and bound by CPI Group (UK) Ltd, Croydon CR0 4YY

*This is for Lucinda and Ben who are forever grateful
to their father for his plans*

CONTENTS

PREFACE

This book is different from most business books. It is a practical workbook that will enable you to prepare your own marketing plan.

In the course of this book, you will follow the development of a marketing plan for a fictitious company – The Equipment Manufacturing Company. Step by step you will be shown how to carry out the different steps in marketing planning. Exercises help you to produce sections of your own marketing plan.

By the time you reach the end of this book, we will have completed our marketing plan and you will have completed yours.

The book can be used in many ways:

- to prepare individual marketing plans;

- as an individual study guide;

- for group marketing planning exercises;

- as a textbook for marketing courses.

Since the completed plan is included at the end of the book, we include the answers as well as the questions!

01
Introduction

Planning is one of the most important roles of management. A company's corporate or business plan runs the business. A company's marketing plan is a key input to the business plan. It should identify the most promising business opportunities for the company and outline how to penetrate, capture and maintain positions in identified markets. It is a communication tool combining all the elements of the marketing mix in a coordinated action plan. It spells out who will do what, when, where and how, to achieve its ends.

An overall company marketing plan can be made up of a number of smaller marketing plans for individual products or areas. These smaller plans can be prepared as and when the occasion requires.

Most books on marketing planning concentrate on theory. This approach is fine for business academics but makes the whole process too complicated for the average sales manager. The approach in this book is a practical one, including only as much theory as is necessary to understand the planning process. Working your way through this book will broaden your understanding of the principles of marketing planning so that you will be able to carry out the background work necessary to put together any type of marketing plan.

It is, however, becoming more common for sales and marketing personnel to have to put together individual plans for a product or an area very quickly. This book is designed as much to help those people as to provide guidance to marketing personnel putting together an overall marketing plan.

Throughout the book we will follow the fortunes of a company manufacturing filters and valves – The Equipment Manufacturing Company. It will be used in examples and as the basis of a marketing plan. The plan will be for all its products for its home market. To get the best out of this book, you should follow this example and prepare an equivalent marketing plan for a product for your own company as we progress through the steps one by one. By the end of the book, you will have your own marketing plan.

Adopting and following the formal structure of the plan (shown later in this book) will make it easier for you to order your thoughts and the facts logically.

It will be easier for:

- people reading the plan to follow your arguments and to see how you reached your conclusions;
- you to present a professional-looking and complete document from even a relatively small amount of information.

The Equipment Manufacturing Company is a medium-sized company based in the south of England. Key facts are given below:

Company name: The Equipment Manufacturing Company

Annual turnover:	£6 m
UK sales:	£2 m
Export sales:	£4 m
Operating profit:	£1.05 m
Number of employees:	65
Main products:	Valves and filters

List the same information below for your own company or business unit:

Company name: _____

Annual turnover: _____

UK sales: _____

Export sales: _____

Operating profit: _____

Number of employees: _____

Main products: _____

Before we proceed, we need to cover some basic definitions. So first of all, answer the following questions:

What is selling?

_____

_____

_____

What is marketing?

_____

_____

_____

What is marketing planning?

_____

_____

_____

Check your answers with the definitions that follow.

What is selling?

Selling is a straightforward concept which involves persuading a customer to buy a product. It brings in 'today's orders'. It is, however, only one aspect of the marketing process.

What is marketing?

The dictionary definition of marketing is: 'the provision of goods or services to meet consumers' needs'. In other words, marketing involves finding out what the customer wants and matching a company's products to meet those requirements, and in the process making a profit for the company. Successful marketing involves having the right product available in the right place at the right time and making sure that the customer is aware of the product. It therefore brings in 'tomorrow's orders'.

It is the process that brings together the abilities of the company and the requirements of its customers. Companies have to be flexible in order to achieve this balance in the marketplace. They must be prepared to change products, introduce new products or enter new markets. They must be able to read their customers and the marketplace. This balancing process takes place in the 'marketing environment' which is not controlled by individuals or by companies, is constantly changing and must be monitored continuously.

Marketing therefore involves:

- the abilities of the company;
- the requirements of the customer;
- the marketing environment.

The abilities of the company can be managed by the marketing function. It can control four main elements of a company's operation, which are often referred to as 'the marketing mix', also known as the 'four Ps'. These are four controllable variables that allow a company to come up with a policy that is profitable and satisfies its customers:

- the product sold (Product);
- the pricing policy (Price);
- how the product is promoted (Promotion);
- methods of distribution (Place).

'Promotion' and 'place' are concerned with reaching your potential customers in the first place, and 'product' and 'price' will allow you to satisfy the customer's requirements.

Exercise

Below we consider the marketing mix for The Equipment Manufacturing Company for the product line 'Standard Filters'.

Standard filters

- *Pricing*

  For this product we have adopted a 'discount policy'. We are offering:

  - discounts for online purchases to encourage the use of our online shop;
  - quantity discounts to encourage larger unit purchases;
  - a discount level for next year based on the level of purchases this year.

- *Promotion*

  For this product, we have adopted the following approach:

  - we advertise this product in the technical press;
  - we have a range of product brochures that can be downloaded from our website;
  - we carry out regular mailshots and e-mailshots.

- *Distribution*

  This product is sold in the UK through our own sales force and independent distributors. It is also available from our online shop. Overseas it is sold through independent distributors.

Consider the marketing mix for your company's products. For each of your main products write some notes on the pricing policy, how the product is promoted and how the product is distributed.

	Product 1	Product 2	Product 3
Pricing	_____	_____	_____
	_____	_____	_____
	_____	_____	_____
Promotion	_____	_____	_____
	_____	_____	_____
	_____	_____	_____
Distribution	_____	_____	_____
	_____	_____	_____
	_____	_____	_____

What is marketing planning?

The term *marketing planning* is used to describe the methods of applying marketing resources to achieve marketing objectives. This may sound simple, but it is in fact a very complex process. The resources and the objectives will vary from company to company and will also change with time. Marketing planning is used to segment markets, identify market position, forecast market size, and to plan viable market share within each market segment.

The process involves:

- carrying out marketing research within and outside the company;
- looking at the company's strengths and weaknesses;
- making assumptions;
- forecasting;
- setting marketing objectives;
- generating marketing strategies;
- defining programmes;
- setting budgets;
- reviewing the results and revising the objectives, strategies or programmes.

Each of these will be discussed individually in later chapters.

The planning process will:

- make better use of company resources to identify marketing opportunities;
- encourage team spirit and company identity;
- help the company to move towards achieving its corporate goals.

In addition, the marketing research carried out as part of the planning process will provide a solid base of information for present and future projects.

Top tip

Marketing planning is an iterative process and plans should be reviewed and updated as they are implemented.

Stages in the preparation of a marketing plan

The stages in the preparation of a marketing plan are shown in Figure 1.1.

Figure 1.1 The marketing planning process

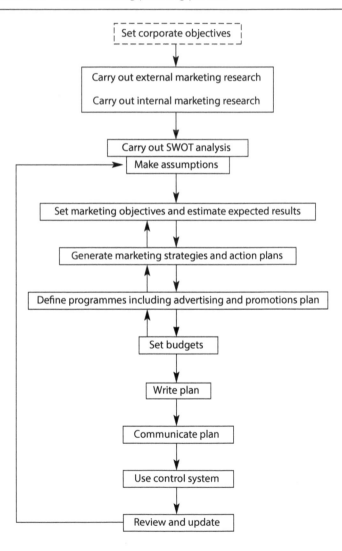

Set corporate objectives

Corporate objectives are set by top management and this may not be in your brief. Even so, you must be aware of your company's corporate objectives and the ultimate plan should be in line with them.

Carry out external marketing research

Since companies exist and operate in the marketing environment, the first step in a marketing plan is research into that environment. Research is carried out into the markets themselves and then the information collected is analysed in the context of the marketing of the products.

Carry out internal marketing research

Perhaps even more important than general market information is historical information available 'in house'. This will be sales/order and margin/profit data relating to the products and areas for the plan. This information needs to be put into context in the form of market shares by geographical area and industry type for individual products and in total.

Carry out SWOT analysis

When all the information and opinions have been collected by market research, the materials need to be analysed and presented in a way that will help to make the best decisions. This can be done by selecting the key information and carrying out a SWOT analysis. The method of carrying out SWOT analysis is explained in detail in Chapter 2.

Make assumptions

The plan itself is based on a clearly understood set of assumptions. These relate to external economic factors as well as technological and competitive factors.

Set marketing objectives and estimate expected results

The next step is the key to the whole marketing process: the setting of marketing objectives. This is what you want to achieve – the fundamental aims of the plan. How to set objectives is covered in Chapter 3.

Generate marketing strategies and action plans

Marketing strategies are the methods that will enable you to achieve your marketing objectives. They relate to the elements of the marketing mix – product, price, promotion and place. For each objective, strategies need to be developed relating to these individual elements. First the marketing strategy needs to be set out and then action plans are prepared. This is covered in Chapter 4.

Define programmes including advertising and promotions plans

Defining programmes means defining who does what, when, where and how.

Set budgets

Objectives can be set and strategies and action plans devised, but they need to be cost-effective. The setting of budgets defines the resources required to carry out the plan and quantifies the cost and also the financial risks involved. It is explained in Chapter 7.

Write plan

Once all the above steps have been carried out you will be in a position to prepare the written plan. The written plan should only contain the key information that needs to be communicated.

Communicate plan

If a plan is not properly communicated to those who will be implementing it, it will fail.

Review and update

Conditions and situations will change and the plan should be regularly reviewed in the light of changing circumstances.

Summary points

Marketing planning involves the application of marketing resources to achieve marketing objectives. It is used to:

- segment markets;
- identify market position;
- forecast market size;
- plan viable market share within each market segment.

02
Situation analysis – the marketing audit

The marketing audit is a detailed examination of the company's marketing environment, specific marketing activities and its internal marketing system. In this chapter we will concentrate on the audit of the marketing environment. We will come back in more detail to the marketing mix and the marketing system in later chapters.

The audit of the marketing environment

This is an examination of the company's markets, customers, competitors and the overall economic and political environment. It involves marketing research and the collecting of historical data about your company and its products. It is an iterative process. It is only when you start to analyse your own in-house data that you realize which market sectors you need to look at outside and once you look at the external data you may notice applications that are small for your company, but larger in a market context and therefore require further investigation.

The audit of marketing activity

This is a study of the company's marketing mix – product, price, promotion and place.

The audit of the marketing system

This involves looking at the current structure of the marketing organization together with its systems.

The marketing environment – market research

At the same time that you consider historical sales data for your company, you need to collect information that will allow it to be put into perspective. This involves market research – collecting information about your markets and then analysing it in the context of the marketing of the products.

Market research is used to:

- give a description of the market;
- monitor how the market changes;
- decide on actions to be taken by a company and evaluate the results of these actions.

Market research data consists of primary data and secondary data. Primary data is data obtained from primary sources, ie directly in the marketplace. This is gathered either by carrying out field research directly yourself or by commissioning a consultant or market research company to carry out the fieldwork for you. Secondary data is not obtained directly from fieldwork, and market research based on secondary data sources is referred to as desk research.

Desk research involves the collection of data from existing sources.

Desk research is usually carried out online. A huge amount of information is available and much of this can be obtained free of charge.

If you want information on milk production, just type in 'milk production' or 'dairy production'. This will get you sites with both data on how to produce milk and sites giving statistical data. So you need to refine your search. Perhaps try 'milk production statistics'. Similarly, if you are really only interested in milk production in Europe or just the United Kingdom, just type in 'milk production + Europe' or 'milk production + UK'.

You can find out a lot about your main competitors by checking out their websites. The 'who are we?' section will often give a potted history of their company and from the 'products' section you will be able to download pdf files of their brochures and datasheets.

Once you have done as much as you can by general web searches, try other sources to get more specific data. These sources could include:

- Government statistics (from the Office of National Statistics, www.ons.gov.uk). Note: most government departments and many other agencies and public bodies have now been merged into GOV.UK, www.gov.uk/government/organisations. (At the time of writing, the Office of National Statistics has its own website – but this may change.)

- Country reports for export markets. These are available from the Department for International Trade (DIT), www.gov.uk/ government/organisations/department-for-international-trade. The Department for International Trade's export home page is www.great.gov.uk. There are direct links to country and business sector reports via the weblinks www.gov.uk/government/ collections/exporting-country-guides and https://www.great. gov.uk/markets.

- Company information (from Companies House, www.gov.uk/ government/organisations/companies-house, or companies such as Kompass, gb.kompass.com).
- Trade directories.
- Trade associations (find details of trade associations for your industry from Trade Association Forum, www.taforum.org).
- Ready-made reports (from companies such as Euromonitor, www.euromonitor.com; Mintel, www.mintel.com; and Frost & Sullivan, ww2.frost.com).
- Industry-specific websites (such as www.essentialchemicalindustry. org for the chemical industry; www.leatherheadfood.com for the food industry).

The market research information for your marketing plan will consist of *market information* and *product information*.

Market information

Market information needs to tell us:

• *The market's size*	How big is it? How is it segmented/structured?
• *Its characteristics*	Who are the main customers? Who are the main suppliers? What are the main products sold?
• *The state of the market*	Is it a new market? A mature market? A saturated market?
• *How well are companies doing?*	Relative to the market as a whole? In relation to each other?
• *Channels of distribution*	What are they?

- *Methods of communication* What methods are used – press, TV, internet, email, social media? What types of sales promotion?

- *Financial* Are there problems caused by: Taxes/duties? Import restrictions?

- *Legal* Patent situation; product standards Legislation relating to agents Trademarks/copyright Protection of intellectual property (designs, software, etc)

- *Developments* What new areas of the market are developing? What new products are developing? Is new legislation or are new regulations likely?

Product information

Product information relates to your own company, your competitors and the customers:

- *Potential customers* Who are they? Where are they located? Who are the market leaders? Do they own competitors?

- *Your own company* Do existing products meet customers' needs? Is product development necessary? Are completely new products required? What would be the potential of a new product? How is your company perceived in the market?

- *Your competitors*   Who are they?

How do they compare with your company in size?

Where are they located?

Do they operate in the same market sectors as you?

What products do they manufacture/sell?

How does their pricing compare with your own?

What sales/distribution channels do they use?

Have they recently introduced new products?

Example

The Equipment Manufacturing Company sets about carrying out external market research. It is looking for information on valves and filters and companies that manufacture them. For this particular marketing plan it is concentrating on the UK market.

It already has a lot of information on valves. The company belongs to the British Valve & Actuator Association (BVAA). The BVAA produces company profiles of all the valve manufacturers in the UK that belong to the Association, together with details of the types of valves that they produce. Our company manufactures ball valves and from the BVAA website we can see that there are six other manufacturers of ball valves in the BVAA. Other companies manufacture other types of valves – diaphragm, gate, butterfly, etc.

Then they check all of their main competitors' websites. These include www.biggsvalves.com and www.sparcovalves.com for their main UK competitors, and www.texasvalves.com and www.dvk.com for their main overseas competitors. They also check out www.dvk.co.uk, which is the UK website of their German competitor DVK. From these websites they are able to download their competitors' mission statements, product literature and information about new products and other developments, such as the establishment of a new distribution centre by DVK.

Next they go to Companies House (www.gov.uk/government/ organisations/companies-house) and use the WebCHeck service to find information including annual reports for their UK competitors. They are able to purchase the reports online and download them as pdf files. The information given varies – small companies do not have to give turnover and divisions of larger companies may have individual reports. Nevertheless a considerable number of companies still show an annual sales split between UK sales and Export sales.

The next source is the Office for National Statistics, www.ons. gov.uk, which produces Prodcom statistics. These are details of the value of production, imports and exports of products for the UK. It uses the Prodcom headings set by Eurostat. The information is normally produced in the form of annual data publications. They type 'valves' into the search engine on the website and it brings up a number of reports. The reports are on 'Product Sales and Trade: Taps and Valves', so they have to separate out the information relating to ball valves. By subtracting imports from exports, and taking this figure from UK production, they are able to establish that the UK market for ball valves is £10 million; they sell £1 million in the UK market. Prodcom statistics also tell them that imports are £4 million, of which £2 million comes from the EU.

Finally, the BVAA advises them that there are a number of published reports by companies like Frost & Sullivan (ww2.frost. com) and small market research companies. They are able to obtain a number of reports including *Pumps and Valves in the Water Industry*, and *A Survey of Equipment Suppliers to the Food Industry*.

They have now been able to establish that the UK market for their product is about £10 million; they have sales of £1 million. Imports are £4 million, of which £2 million comes from the EU. From this data they can produce a table showing UK market shares (see Table 2.1).

Table 2.1   Market share information

UK market share – ball valves		
Company	£k	%
Equipment Mfg	1,000	10
Biggs Valves	2,200	22
Sparco Valves	800	8
DVK (German)	1,600	16
Texas Valves (US)	800	8
Others	3,600	36
Total	10,000	100

Exercise

Now consider the product(s) and area(s) that you will use for your marketing plan. Follow through the same exercise that we have just carried out for The Equipment Manufacturing Company. Start by using the internet to track down information relating to your market and your competitors. Do you have a trade association? If so, contact them and see what information they have. Also contact your local Chamber of Commerce. Put together as much information as you can on the products, the markets, competition, market shares, etc.

Internal market research

In addition to the external market research, your company has a wealth of data that is invaluable in the preparation of a marketing plan. In fact the problem is more likely to be that there is too much data so that you cannot easily see which information is the most important. It is likely that much data will not be available in the right form. You may have overall sales data, but not data itemized for individual product lines or market segments.

The historical data relevant to the preparation of your marketing plan is basically sales/order data separated and analysed in such a way that it reflects the key market segments into which you sell your products.

What is market segmentation?

Different customers have different needs. They do not all require the same product and they do not all require the same product benefits. Even with an individual product, not all customers will buy it for the same reasons.

Top tip

Market segmentation allows you to consider:

• the markets you are actually in;

• the markets that your company should be in.

You need to be able to split your customer base up into groups of customers who all have similar needs. Each of these groups constitutes a market segment.

For consumer goods and services, it is usual to classify the end- users by the use of methods of classification which separate consumers by socio-economic group, age, sex, occupation or region.

The marketing of industrial goods is different from services. Because the customer is usually another company or a government department, the number of customers is more likely to be ten thousand than ten million and could be only a few hundred in the case of suppliers to power stations, coal mines, etc.

The main ways of defining segments here are by:

- geographical area;
- industry or industry subsector;
- product;
- application;
- size of end-user;
- distribution channel – distributor, equipment manufacturer, end-user.

Segmentation can also be based on:

- order size;
- order frequency;
- type of decision-maker.

The key to market segmentation is to let the marketplace segment itself, because the individual segments exist independently of the company and its products.

For the products and markets covered by your plan, you should collect and present information going back two or three full years together with this year's historical sales. You should show margin information relating to those sales, where it is available. You should also adjust figures for inflation and have them available in their actual and adjusted forms.

Information checklist

It is useful to prepare an information checklist for a marketing plan before you start to collect data. The exact content will vary, depending on the scope of your plan, but it should include details of the segmentation that you want for sales, the split of your customer base, and competitor activity/market shares. The detail of the information will vary depending on the type of company, and this will mean that details listed in the checklist will also vary and should be customized to your company.

In order to prepare a marketing plan for the UK market for all its products The Equipment Manufacturing Company has put together a checklist of information required (shown below).

---

1 **Sales history**

The last three years' sales by value (including margins where available) for:

- sales areas: South, Midlands, North, Wales, Scotland/NI;
- product groups: ball valves, type 'S', type 'A' and type 'K' filters, packages;
- main equipment and spares.

Also unit sales:

- number of valves by model size;
- number of filters by model size.

2 **Customers**

Total number of customers by:

- sales area: South, Midlands, North, Wales, Scotland/NI;
- products bought: ball valves, type 'S', type 'A' and type 'K' filters, packages;
- market: chemical/petrochemical, water treatment, paper, food;
- key customers, ie top 40 by sales turnover.

3 **Competition**

- Who are the competitors for each product group?
- What are the market shares for each product for each competitor?

Now prepare an information checklist for your own company for the products and areas to be covered by your plan.

Information checklist

1 Sales history

Prepare last three years' sales by:

_____

_____

_____

2 Customers

Segment customers by:

_____

_____

_____

3 Competition

How do we want to present competitor information?

_____

_____

_____

How to present the figures

Depending on the scope of the plan, the sales data may be split up into separate tables geographically, by product, by industry or under all of these categories.

The figures can easily be prepared on computer spreadsheets such as Microsoft's Excel or Apple's Numbers for Mac. These programs have the facility for the data entered into the spreadsheet tables to be displayed graphically as well. It is usual when producing tables of historical data on a spreadsheet to extend the form layout to include columns for the years which the marketing plan will cover. The columns for future years will remain blank at this time as the current task is to record historical and current sales data, but it makes it easier later on to project sales figures so that comparisons can be made and trends can be seen.

Table 2.2 shows how the figures could be presented for The Equipment Manufacturing Company for use in their UK marketing plan.

Table 2.2 Sales figures UK (all products)

The Equipment Manufacturing Company sales figures						
Sales area: UK						
	←——Actual——→			←—— Forecast ——→		
Year (all values in £k)	**20X3**	**20X4**	**20X5**	**20X6**	**20X7**	**20X8**
Filters	200	450	600			
Valves	1,400	1,200	1,000			
Components	300	350	400			
Total	1,900	2,000	2,000			

Inflation over the past three years has been 3 per cent per year. This information therefore needs to be adjusted for inflation (Table 2.3).

Table 2.3   Sales figures UK (adjusted for inflation)

The Equipment Manufacturing Company sales figures						
Sales area: UK						
	←——— Actual ———→			←——— Forecast ———→		
Year (all values in £k)	**20X3**	**20X4**	**20X5**	**20X6**	**20X7**	**20X8**
Filters	200	437	566			
Valves	1,400	1,165	943			
Components	300	340	377			
Total	1,900	1,942	1,886			

Another way to look at volume growth is to analyse unit sales rather than sales value (Table 2.4).

Table 2.4   Unit sales of filters

The Equipment Manufacturing Company sales figures						
Sales area: UK						
Product: Filters						
	←——— Actual ———→			←——— Forecast ———→		
Year (number of units)	**20X3**	**20X4**	**20X5**	**20X6**	**20X7**	**20X8**
Type S	402	396	412			
Type A	100	120	140			
Type K	50	100	150			
Packages	4	8	14			
Total	556	624	716			

The profitability of sales is very important. It is therefore necessary also to show the margins being made on the sale of different products (Table 2.5).

Table 2.5   Sales figures for the UK including margin information

The Equipment Manufacturing Company sales figures						
Sales area: UK						
Year	**20X3**		**20X4**		**20X5**	
	Sales £k	**Gross profit %**	**Sales £k**	**Gross profit %**	**Sales £k**	**Gross profit %**	**Comments**
Filters	200	40	450	40	600	40	
Valves	1,400	30	1,200	30	1,000	30	
Components	300	60	350	60	400	60	
Total	1,900	35.8	2,000	37.5	2,000	39	

More detailed information should also be shown for the main geographical areas of the plan (Table 2.6).

Table 2.6   Sales figures for valves in the UK

The Equipment Manufacturing Company sales						
Sales area: UK						
Product: Valves						
	← Actual →			← Forecast →		
Year (number of units)	**20X3**	**20X4**	**20X5**	**20X6**	**20X7**	**20X8**
South	295	250	230			
Midlands	485	415	360			
North	525	420	300			
Wales	45	55	60			
Scotland/NI	50	60	50			
Total	1,400	1,200	1,000			

This information could also be shown graphically as in Figures 2.1 and 2.2.

Figure 2.1   Sales figures for valves in the UK

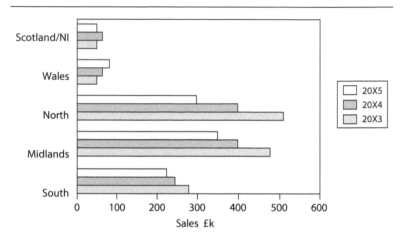

Figure 2.2   UK sales by product

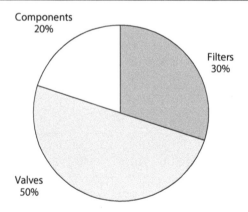

Now prepare a similar set of data for your product for your own example plan. It is important that you carry out the exercise even if you do not have all the data available to complete all of the tables.

Situation analysis

Completing the market research and collecting the historical data about your company and its products is only the first step. You need to analyse this information and present it in a way that can be used for planning. Situation analysis is a process which helps you do this. It:

- reviews the economic and business climate;
- considers where the company stands in its strategic markets and key sales areas;
- looks at the strengths and weaknesses of the company – its organization, its performance and its key products;
- compares the company with its competitors;
- identifies opportunities and threats.

The results of this analysis are included in the marketing plan under the following headings:

- Assumptions.
- Sales.
- Strategic or key markets.
- Key products.
- Key sales areas.

SWOT analysis

The key process used in situation analysis is SWOT analysis.

> ## Top tip
>
> SWOT stands for:
>
> *Strengths and Weaknesses as they relate to our Opportunities and Threats in the marketplace.*

The strengths and weaknesses refer to the company and its products whereas the opportunities and threats are usually taken to be external factors over which your company has no control. SWOT analysis involves understanding and analysing your strengths and weaknesses and identifying threats to your business as well as opportunities in the marketplace. You can then attempt to exploit your strengths, overcome your weaknesses, grasp your opportunities and defend yourself against threats. This is one of the most important parts of the planning process. SWOT analysis asks the questions that will enable you to decide whether your company and the product will really be able to fulfil your plan and what the constraints will be.

In carrying out SWOT analysis it is usual to list the strengths, weaknesses, opportunities and threats on the same page. This is done by segmenting the page into four squares and entering strengths and weaknesses in the top squares and opportunities and threats in the bottom squares, as shown in Figure 2.3.

The number of individual SWOTs will depend on the scope of your plan. First you should carry out a SWOT on your company and its organization. You should also do the same for your main competitors and for your products, geographical areas and market segments covered by the plan.

Figure 2.3   Presentation of SWOT analysis

Strengths	Weaknesses
Opportunities	Threats

Example

The following figures show a number of SWOT analyses that The Equipment Manufacturing Company has prepared and will use in its UK marketing plan.

Figures 2.4, 2.5, 2.6, 2.7, 2.8 and 2.9 show SWOTs on the company, its sales organization, a product, a sales area, a market segment and a competitor.

Figure 2.4   Company SWOT analysis

Strengths	Weaknesses
• Part of large UK Group • Good image – quality company • Good resources – financial, technical • Established export sales	• Sales in UK are not growing • Thought of as 'old fashioned' • Few marketing staff • Website needs updating and expanding
Opportunities	**Threats**
• Parent company is investing in new marketing department • New Group R&D facility • To develop new products	• Low-priced products from the Far East • Niche products from EU countries

Figure 2.5 Sales organization SWOT analysis

Strengths	Weaknesses
• Large field sales force in UK • Have industry specialists • New modern offices	• Many new staff – need experience • Staff training required
Opportunities	**Threats**
• To recruit new sales manager • To restructure sales force • To carry out advanced sales training	• No in-house successor to sales and marketing director • Competitors expanding field sales forces

Figure 2.6 SWOT analysis for product – ball valves

Strengths	Weaknesses
• Good range of sizes • Quality product • Solidly built	• Limited range of materials • Heavier than competitors' products • High cost/high price
Opportunities	**Threats**
• Source product from China • Develop new product	• Cheap imports from Asia • Competing products in plastic materials

Figure 2.7 SWOT analysis for a geographical sales area – the North of England

Strengths	Weaknesses
• Large industrial base • Industrial sites concentrated in a few areas	• Many old plants • Not many new projects • All major competitors present
Opportunities	**Threats**
• Refurbish old plants • Diversify into new industries, eg water treatment	• Biggs' strongest area • More companies are moving production abroad • More companies may shut for good

Figure 2.8   SWOT analysis for a market segment – water industry

Strengths	Weaknesses
• Strong with filters • We have an industry expert	• A 'lowest price' market • Weak with valves • No economies of scale
Opportunities • New investment programme for the UK water industry • New products, eg motorized timer valve	**Threats** • No longer 'buy British' bias • Some water companies now owned by foreign companies (French/German/US) • Some competitors can package products together • Water company owned competitors

Figure 2.9   SWOT analysis for a competitor – DVK (Germany)

Their strengths	Their weaknesses
• Large company • Wide product range • Relatively high market share • Good name	• Just sacked distributor • Inexperienced own sales force • Lack service support • Old fashioned product
Opportunities for us • Ball valves are manufactured in a high-cost factory in Germany • New product developments	**Threats to us** • They may set up a service support organization • They are building a low-cost factory in China

Exercise

Now consider your own sample plan and carry out SWOTs in the same format for:

• your company;

• your sales organization;

- each of your key products;
- each of your key sales areas;
- each of your key market segments;
- each of your major competitors.

Strengths	Weaknesses
Opportunities	Threats

With the completion of the situation analysis we are now ready to move on to setting objectives and deciding strategies.

Summary points

After carrying out external market research and adding your own 'in-house' data you need to analyse the information and present it in a way that can be used for planning. Situation analysis helps you to:

- consider where your company stands in its strategic markets and key sales areas;
- look at your company's strengths and weaknesses;
- compare your company with your competitors;
- identify opportunities and threats.

03
Objectives

Now that we have identified our key strengths and weaknesses, the opportunities and threats to our business, and made assumptions about outside factors that may affect our business, we are in a position to set our marketing objectives. This is the key step in the whole process of preparing a marketing plan.

What is a marketing objective?

Top tip

- Objectives are what we want to achieve.
- Strategies are how we get there.

A marketing objective concerns the balance between products and their markets. It relates to *which products* we want to sell into *which markets*. The means of achieving these objectives, using price, promotion and distribution are marketing strategies. At the next level down there will be personnel objectives and personnel strategies, advertising objectives and advertising strategies, etc. There will then be tactics, action plans and budgets – all to enable us to achieve our objectives.

Marketing objectives relate to any of the following:

- selling existing products into existing markets;
- selling existing products into new markets;

- selling new products into existing markets;
- selling new products into new markets.

Marketing objectives should always be **SMART**:

- **Specific** – they should be expressed in terms of values or market shares, and vague terms such as increase, improve or maximize should not be used.

- **Measurable** – you should be able to confirm whether you have achieved them or not.

- **Achievable** – do you have the resources, in terms of people and investment, to achieve them?

- **Realistic** – although targets should be stretching, if they are clearly unrealistic, they will just be demotivating.

- **Time-bound** – there should be a set timescale for achieving every objective.

The following are examples of marketing objectives:

- to increase sales of the product in the UK by 10 per cent per annum in real terms, each year for the next three years;
- to increase sales of the product worldwide by 30 per cent in real terms within five years;
- to increase market share for the product in the United States from 10 per cent to 15 per cent over two years.

You need to have short-term as well as long-term objectives. Increasing sales by 30 per cent over five years may seem a huge rise, but if you redefine it as increasing sales by 5 or 6 per cent a year, it will appear to be much more achievable.

Below are listed some preliminary objectives of The Equipment Manufacturing Company:

- to increase UK sales by 10 per cent per year in real terms for the next three years;
- to double ball valve sales to the water industry within three years;

- to increase sales of packages to 50 units within three years;
- to double market share for filters in the water industry by 20X8;
- to double distributor sales in Scotland and NI by 20X8;
- to increase overall gross margins from 39 per cent to 43 per cent by 20X8.

Exercise

Now make a preliminary list of some marketing objectives that you think would be sensible for your sample plan.

_____

_____

In all plans, marketing objectives for the following should be set:

- sales turnover for the period of the plan by product and market segment;
- gross profit on sales;
- market share for the period of the plan by product and market segment, where possible.

Basic types of product

Top tip

From a marketing point of view there are three basic types of products:

- Consumer goods.
- Industrial goods.
- Services.

There are, of course, some products that could be in all three categories. Paint is an example. It can be purchased by both consumers and industrial companies and it can also be part of the 'service offering' given by a house decorating company. It is also true that not all industrial goods are capital goods and that some consumer goods such as houses or cars are capital items to the purchaser. Nevertheless, these broad definitions hold in most cases and key marketing principles apply equally to the marketing of consumer goods, capital goods and services. It is just the way that the principles are applied that takes a different form.

Consumer goods

Consumer markets are characterized by having a large number of customers. By their very nature consumer goods are usually items that are mass-produced in identical form. There are two basic types of consumer goods: fast moving consumer goods and consumer durables.

Fast moving consumer goods – sometimes called convenience goods. These are items such as food, drinks and cosmetics that have a quick turnover and tend to be quickly consumed.

Consumer durables – these are items such as cars, furniture, clothing and electrical goods which are less frequent purchases that will be used by the customer for a long time.

Industrial goods

Industrial goods are any goods sold by industrial companies to manufacturers, suppliers, contractors or government agencies. The goods would normally be incorporated into other products, used within the company's own business or resold. Industrial goods can be raw materials, components or capital goods. The ultimate consumer of the final product probably has little interest in the raw materials or components used in its manufacture. Capital goods are often sold directly to the end-user – with the exception of direct online sales by the manufacturer this is almost never the case with consumer goods which are usually sold through complex distribution networks.

Services

The third basic type of product is a service. By this we do not mean the customer service that most reputable companies supply with their products, but a service as a product in its own right.

Services range from financial services such as banking and insurance to car hire and carrying out computer repairs. They differ from consumer and industrial goods in that in a service industry there is no tangible product and the product has no shelf life. Service organizations sell the benefits of their service as their product. This is an important fact, which influences the way in which services are marketed.

The product portfolio

Since marketing objectives relate to *products* and *markets* it is important to understand your present position with regard to both before setting the objectives of your marketing plan.

The growth and decline of all products follows a life cycle curve which can be represented as in Figure 3.1.

Figure 3.1   Product life cycle curve

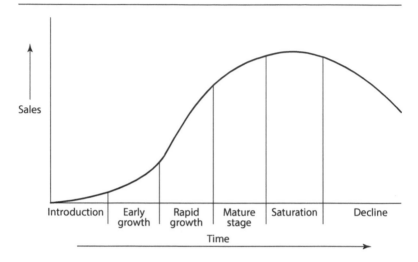

Figure 3.2   A product portfolio

Ideally your company will have a portfolio of products, all at different stages in their life cycle, so that balanced growth can be achieved and risks minimized. Figure 3.2 shows a typical product portfolio.

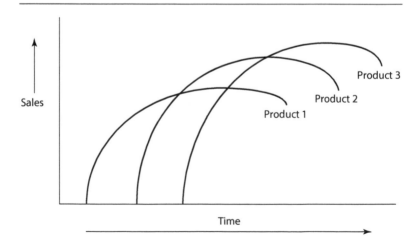

Figures 3.3 and 3.4 show product portfolio curves for the main products manufactured by The Equipment Manufacturing Company.

The 'type S' filters have reached the 'saturation' stage of their life cycle, 'type A' filters are at the 'mature' stage of development and 'type K' filters and packages are at the 'rapid' stage of growth.

Ball valves are a problem, since they are already in the stage of 'decline'. Products at this stage of their development will start to decline even more quickly unless something is done. The long-term requirement would be to develop a new product, but it is often possible to give a product a new, albeit short, lease of life. In the case of The Equipment Manufacturing Company, this is perhaps possible by combining the ball valves with filters in packages for the water treatment industry.

Figure 3.3 Product portfolio for The Equipment Manufacturing Company for filters

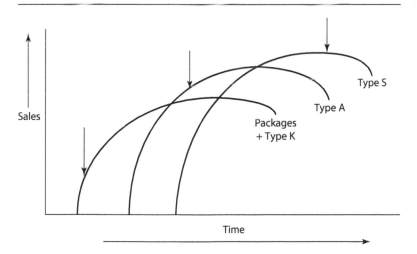

Figure 3.4   Product portfolio for The Equipment Manufacturing
Company for ball valves

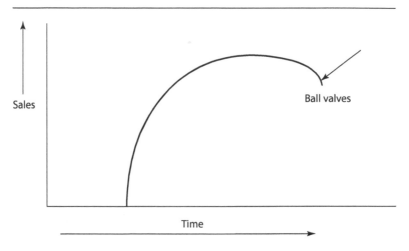

Exercise

Now construct life cycle/product portfolio curves (Figure 3.5) for
your company's products and indicate where they are currently
on these curves.

Figure 3.5   Product portfolio exercise

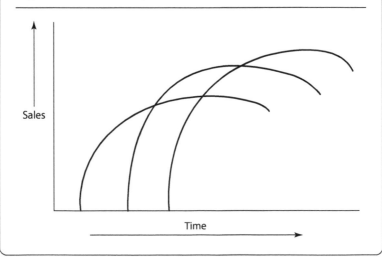

Relative market growth rate and share

In any market the price levels of the major players tend to be broadly similar. In a stable market the price levels of the major players will gradually move together. This does not mean that all these companies will make the same level of profit. If one company has a very large market share, it will benefit from economies of scale and will have lower costs. The company with the highest market share is likely to have the highest profit margin. It is therefore more able to withstand a price war. Its market share also indicates its ability to generate cash. Market share is therefore very important and it should be your aim to achieve market dominance wherever possible.

Cash flow is the most important factor in considering your product portfolio, and your company's ability to generate cash will be dependent, to a large extent, on the degree of market dominance that you have over your competitors.

Some years ago the Boston Consulting Group developed a matrix for classifying a portfolio of products based on relative market shares and relative market growth rates. The 'Boston Matrix' is now widely used by companies to consider their product portfolio.

The products are colourfully described as:

Stars – high market share/high market growth (cash neutral).

Cash cows – high market share/low market growth (cash generation).

Question marks – low market share/high market growth (cash drain).

Dogs – low market share/low market growth (cash neutral).

Relative market share is the ratio of your market share to the market share of your biggest competitor. It indicates the level of market dominance that you have over your competitors.

Market growth rate is important for two reasons. In a fast-growing market the sales of a product can grow more quickly than in a slow-growing or stable market. In increasing sales, the product will absorb a high level of cash to support increasing advertising, sales coverage, sales support and possibly even investment in additional plant and machinery. For the purposes of marketing planning, high market growth is normally taken as 10 per cent per annum or more.

The products are entered into the quadrants of the matrix as shown in Figure 3.6.

Question marks can be either newly launched products which have not yet fulfilled expectation, or products that are declining and need further evaluation as to their long-term viability.

Dogs have low market share and are generally unprofitable. These products would be considered as those that could be dropped from the product portfolio.

Figure 3.6   Ideal product development sequence

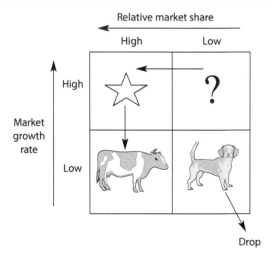

Stars have a high cost in spending on marketing and research and development, but also contribute considerably to profits. They are broadly speaking neutral from the point of view of cash generation.

Cash cows are mature products with a high market share, but low market growth. They generate high profits and require only a small amount of marketing investment and no research and development spending to keep them where they are.

Exercise

Figure 3.7 shows the current position of the product portfolio of The Equipment Manufacturing Company.

The 'type S' filters and 'ball valves' are both cash cows, but ball valves are declining in both relative market share and becoming less and less profitable. 'Packages' are question marks, but will become stars if they continue to grow in relative market share as the market for them expands. 'Type A' and 'type K' filters are both moving into the star sector, with 'type A' a little ahead of 'type K'.

Figure 3.7   Portfolio matrix of The Equipment Manufacturing Company

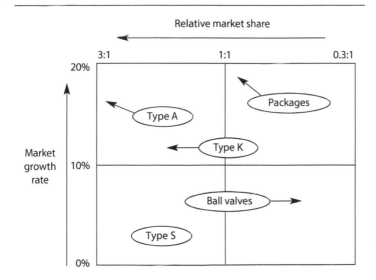

Do similar calculations for the products in your product portfolio and mark them on the matrix in Figure 3.8.

Figure 3.8   Portfolio matrix for your products

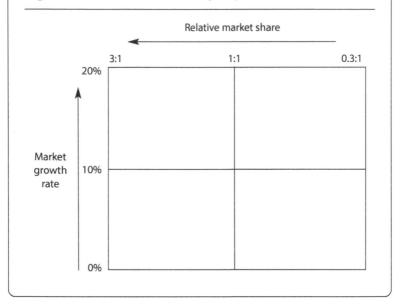

The market portfolio – increasing available markets

As well as looking at your product portfolio, you also need to look at your 'market portfolio'. This is a list of your key markets and key sales areas. You need to consider how you can increase the number of markets and sales areas that you are selling your products into, because this will increase the total potential market for your products. If you have good products that are selling well in your existing markets, this can be a less risky option than developing and launching new products.

Application selling

Application selling is a market development technique that has been used widely in recent years. It involves finding a successful application for your product and promoting this successful application in other geographical areas or in other industries. It applies more to industrial products and services than to consumer products.

A company selling filtration equipment to customers in the food industry may actually only have major sales in the dairy industry. They may be able to increase their business by selling the same product into other industries where the same type of filtration is required, such as the wider food industry or the pharmaceutical industry. They could also capitalize on their success in their domestic market to develop sales in new markets overseas. This is where application selling comes in.

The concept

Application selling can generate additional business for you by:

- Finding more customers in sales areas where you are already selling your product(s) into a particular application.

- Finding potential customers in sales areas where you are either selling very little or selling none of your product(s) into this application.

- Finding potential customers in sales areas handled by your distributors.

- Finding potential customers overseas in areas handled by your distributors.

- Helping you to understand more fully your customers' requirements and consider modifications or improvements to your product or even new products for this particular application.

Preparation of key material

The first step is to identify successful applications that your company has and the products that you are selling for these applications. Because of the investment in time and effort, it is more cost-effective to prepare material for a number of different applications at the same time. Once you have your list and it has been trimmed down to no more than five applications, there are a number of key steps to be followed to prepare the material that you need for each of these applications:

- Obtain information relating to the market size for the industry.
- Analyse your own sales by area, region, etc.
- Put together a list of your actual applications in this industry or industry sector.
- Where applicable put together a simple flow diagram for the process where your product is being used.
- Put together a reference list of customers using your product in this application.
- Use your sales force to obtain site photographs of your equipment installed. (For this you need to get the customer's permission or perhaps, if you have good contacts, they will take the photographs for you.)
- Collect information from competitors' websites of products that they manufacture that compete with yours. From this prepare SWOT analyses of how you and your product compare with them and theirs.
- List out the key benefits that you offer the customer.

Several of these steps will require input from your key sales personnel.

Once you have prepared this material, you need to use it to put together a set of tools that can be used to train both your own sales force and your distributor's sales forces to sell your product into the chosen applications.

Not only do you need to prepare the training material, you also need to carry out structured training as part of an action plan for growing sales in the application. For overseas non-English speaking markets, the material needs to be sent out prior to the training so that it can be translated into the local language.

The package of sales support material will usually consist of the following:

- **An Application Manual.** This documents all the key information on the application – the industry, the size of the market, the application itself, the benefits you are selling to the customer, references, application photos as well as details of your main competitors and their competing products. This is usually a word document containing material that will be used in the presentations.

- **A Training Presentation.** This is a PowerPoint presentation to be used in training your own salesforce and your distributors. It contains details of the industry market, the applications, the benefits to the customer, references, application photos, details of your main competitors together with a SWOT analysis of your competitors for the product used in the application.

- **A Customer Presentation.** This is also a PowerPoint presentation and is used by your salesforce and your distributors' salesforces to make presentations to customers. It contains most of the material from the training presentation, except for the competition material, and in addition it contains key information and benefits for the products you are proposing.

- In some cases additional sales leaflets, data sheets or flyers may also be required.

This may sound like a lot of material to prepare, but bear in mind that much of the material is common between the different documents. Since the documents are available electronically, this means that your overseas distributors can quickly produce versions in their own languages, both for training and presentation purposes.

Exporting

Any company that has good products and a steady level of business in its domestic market should logically consider exporting as a way of growing its business still further. The risks are greater, but the rewards can also be greater. If your company has been successfully selling its products in its domestic market, there is a good chance that it will also be successful in overseas markets – at least in those overseas markets where similar needs and conditions exist. Selling overseas may be more difficult, but at least you are selling something that you know you have sold successfully at home.

Top tip

Why should you consider exporting, rather than just trying to expand your sales in your domestic market? There are two very good reasons:

- Exporting expands your available market.
- No other business activity receives so much encouragement and support.

The potential market

According to the World Bank, the size of the world economy in 2019 was $88 trillion. Although it fell to $85 trillion in 2020 (with the pandemic), it recovered again in 2021. For any company anywhere in the world the potential export market for their product is much larger than their potential domestic market.

The benefits of exporting

According to the Department for International Trade, www.gov.uk/government/organisations/department-for-international-trade, companies that export:

- Improve their productivity.
- Achieve levels of growth not possible domestically.
- Increase the resilience of their revenues and profits.
- Achieve economies of scale not possible domestically.
- Increase the commercial lifespan of their products and services.
- Increase the returns on their investment in R&D.
- Improve their financial performance.
- Feel the benefit.

Exporting can help companies to increase their potential market, increase their turnover, improve their business's reputation, avoid being over dependent on their domestic sales and provide a buffer to any cyclical deterioration in their domestic economy. By finding export markets in different hemispheres, agricultural suppliers can even out seasonal fluctuations in the demand for their products. By working with international clients and partners companies gain knowledge of different cultural environments and get a better insight into their customers' requirements. They gain exposure to new technologies and ideas and also experience a wider range of competitors. This gives them the opportunity to develop new and improved products and services, which can help them to gain and retain competitiveness at home as well as overseas.

Gap analysis

Setting objectives for a marketing plan is not an easy task. Figures for sales turnover or market share cannot just be selected at random. It is an iterative process whereby objectives are set, strategies and action plans are developed, and then it is decided whether the planned objectives are impossible, achievable or easy. The objectives are then reappraised and should they be changed, the strategies and action plans would also need to be re-examined.

At the start of this chapter we set some preliminary objectives for The Equipment Manufacturing Company for their UK plan.

The main objective stated with regard to growth was to increase UK sales by 10 per cent per year for the next three years. Is it a sensible objective? In view of the lack of any growth at all in the last three years it is ambitious. It is more likely to be achievable than 20 per cent growth per year. It takes time for new strategies and plans to work. Most marketing plans therefore show more growth in years two and three than in the first year.

We can use gap analysis to decide how realistic our objectives are.

Top tip

Gap analysis is a technique with many uses. From the point of view of setting marketing objectives it can be used to help you analyse and close the gap between what your company needs to achieve and what is likely to be achieved if policies are unchanged.

Figure 3.9 shows the original and required sales forecast for a company with the gap to be bridged.

For The Equipment Manufacturing Company the figures for the last three years show no growth at all in the UK market. In our assumptions, we estimate that inflation will be running at 3 per cent in 20X6, 4 per cent in 20X7 and 4 per cent in 20X8. Real growth of 10 per cent per year will therefore produce a 'gap' of £937,000 between the required and originally projected growth. (This figure is based on £2 million × 1.13 × 1.14 × 1.14.) The sales projection for The Equipment Manufacturing Company for the UK plan is shown in Table 3.1.

Figure 3.9   A revised sales forecast showing required and originally projected growth

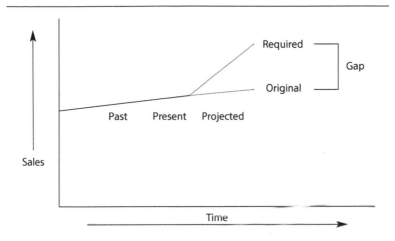

Table 3.1   Sales projection for the UK

The Equipment Manufacturing Company sales figures (historical and forecast)					
Sales area: UK					
	← Actual →			← Forecast →	
Year (all values in £k)	**20X3**	**20X4**	**20X5**	**20X6**	**20X7**	**20X8**
Filters	200	450	600	750	900	1,050
Valves	1,400	1,200	1,000	1,060	1,151	1,287
Components	300	350	400	450	525	600
Total	1,900	2,000	2,000	2,260	2,576	2,937

The next stage is to break this gap down into its constituent parts. Firstly we split it into inflationary growth (price increase) and volume growth.

gap   = £937,000
price increase = £235,000
volume increase = £684,000

If we can double ball valve sales in the water industry this will add:

£300,000 − £150,000 = £150,000

If we can treble sales of packages this will add:

£500,000 − £140,000 = £360,000

We also intend to double filter sales to the water industry. This would add £400,000, but £360,000 of this is already included in 'packages'. Since component sales are basically spare filter cartridges, sales will certainly increase by more than £40,000 as a result of the number of packages sold. The objective 'to double filter sales to the water industry' can therefore be increased. The increase in component sales will be about £150,000.

Doubling sales in Scotland/NI will also add £50,000 to turnover.

This translates into:

price increase   = £235,000
ball valves – water = £150,000
packages   = £360,000
filter cartridges   = £150,000
sales Scotland/NI = £50,000
total increase   = £945,000

Our objectives would therefore close the gap, but only just. It is always wise to have something in reserve, since not all strategies and action plans will bring in the full return that we expect from them.

Summary points

Before setting your marketing objectives, it is important to understand your present position with regard to your products and markets:

- your marketing objectives should be definable and quantifiable;
- they should be expressed in terms of values or market shares;
- they should be challenging, but achievable;
- there should be a set timescale for achieving each objective.

04
Strategies and action plans

What is a marketing strategy?

Marketing strategies are the means by which marketing objectives will be achieved. It is important to understand what strategy is and how it differs from tactics.

Top tip

Strategies are the broad methods chosen to achieve specific objectives. They describe the means of achieving the objectives in the time-scale required. They do not include the detail of the individual courses of action that will be followed on a day-to-day basis: these are *tactics*.

Marketing strategies relate to general policies for the following:

- Products
  - changing product portfolio/mix;
  - dropping, adding or modifying products;
  - changing design, quality or performance;
  - consolidating/standardizing.

- Price
  - changing price, terms or conditions for particular product groups in particular market segments;
  - skimming policies;
  - penetration policies;
  - discount policies.
- Promotion
  - changing selling/salesforce organization;
  - changing advertising or sales promotion;
  - changing public relations policy;
  - increasing/decreasing exhibition coverage.
- Distribution
  - changing channels;
  - improving service.

There are a number of different types of strategies:

- *Defensive strategies* – designed to prevent loss of existing customers;
- *Developing strategies* – designed to offer existing customers a wider range of your products or services;
- *Attacking strategies* – designed to generate business through new customers.

A useful way of looking at the types of strategy that may be available is to use a matrix that was developed by Ansoff, as shown in Figure 4.1.

Figure 4.1 Ansoff matrix – the risks of various strategies

		Low risk	High risk
		Present product	New product
Low risk	Present market	Expand existing market with existing product	Develop new products for existing markets
High risk	New market	Sell present product in new markets	Develop or acquire new products to sell into new markets

It can be seen from this matrix that the least risky way to try to expand your business is in the areas you know best – ie with your existing products in your existing markets.

Pricing strategies

There are many types of pricing strategies and tactics that can be considered. Most can, however, be broadly classified as either skimming policies or penetration policies.

- *Skimming* – this involves entering the market at a high price level and 'skimming' off as much profit as possible. As competition enters the market, the price level would be adjusted as necessary.

- *Penetration* – this is the opposite of skimming. With this type of strategy a company sets the price low deliberately. A penetration policy encourages more customers to purchase the product, which increases the company's sales turnover and also its market share.

Customer strategies

Most companies lose between 10 and 20 per cent of their customers each year. So if you are not planning how you can find new customers or planning for new or enhanced products to meet your existing customers' needs, you will soon be out of business. If you want to be truly proactive you should use strategies like key account management to safeguard your largest and most important accounts.

Customer relationship management

Customer relationship management (CRM) is a widely used strategy for managing a company's interactions with its customers and its sales prospects. It involves using technology to organize, automate and synchronize business processes. Although this relates principally to sales activities, it usually also includes marketing, customer service and technical support. The main purpose of CRM is to assist a company in finding, attracting and winning new clients, as well as retaining those that it already has and winning back former clients that it has lost. Effective CRM should also reduce a company's marketing and client service costs.

CRM systems are designed to:

- manage a company's sales team;
- track its customer data;
- deliver better service.

Major suppliers of CRM software are: Salesforce, Microsoft, SAP and Oracle. Many CRM suppliers offer cloud computing and software as a service (SaaS), which are accessed via a secure internet connection and are sold as subscriptions so that the customers do not need to invest in purchasing and maintaining IT hardware. Subscription costs of these types of packages are much lower than the cost of purchasing software outright.

Salesforce is a major supplier of cloud-based CRM systems with more than 150,000 customers around the world. They were voted Forbes' World's Most Innovative Company from 2011 to 2015 and again in 2017. They provide their CRM software applications as a pay-as-you-go service over the internet. The software is designed to make it easy to customize the application to fit the specific needs of individual customers and industries. Upgrades to the latest version of the software are automatic and are included in the subscription package. Users can log on from anywhere, view and update customer data and work with colleagues at any time of the day or night. All customer information is in one place and is protected with physical security, data encryption, user authentication and application security. The software allows users to capture phone, email and web leads and send them on automatically to the right person to follow up. The system is protected by firewall protection and intrusion detection systems.

Key account management

Most companies have a small number of 'key' customers that make up a large part of their turnover. The loss of any one of these accounts to the competition would have a significant impact on the company's turnover (and profitability). This is why many companies use key account management to develop and improve the working relationship with their most important customers. CRM is ideal for managing the bulk of your customers, but your 'key' customers need something more. Key account management is not just a sales and marketing strategy – it is a company strategy. It involves all major functions within your company, including manufacturing, quality assurance, engineering and logistics.

Key account management is based on building up an understanding of your key customers and their needs. You need to understand why they buy your product and why they buy from your company. You need to understand what their needs are, both in terms of the product and the support/service. You need to make sure that at every level in your company you are providing them with high quality support and immediately reacting to any problems or difficulties they may have. You need to make them so happy with your company and its products that they would not even think of looking for another supplier/product. Also, involving your key account customers in your product development ensures that any new products that you bring out will satisfy their needs both now and in the future.

The Equipment Manufacturing Company has a key account management programme. Their top five domestic customers account for over 30 per cent of their annual domestic turnover. They have a key account management group consisting of the sales director, engineering director, production director, finance/logistics director and the quality assurance manager. When the key account programme was set up three years ago, this group arranged one or two day meetings with each of their top five domestic customers to discuss what they did and didn't like about the company and its products and what could be improved. They took away the results of the discussions and implemented changes where necessary. Six months later they had a follow up progress meeting with these key accounts and subsequently they meet with them once a year. These meetings are not of course the only meetings with these key accounts. There is contact at all levels in the company and visits are made when required. This may sound like a huge commitment, but the really hard work was in the first twelve months. The relationships between the companies have grown to such an extent that if there is now a problem a contact in the key account just phones or emails their counterpart at The Equipment Manufacturing Company.

Devising strategies

For any project there will undoubtedly be many strategies that could be used, so you need to narrow these down by considering only those strategies that offer the greatest chance of success. All of the strategies should be consistent with each other and with the objectives that they are expected to achieve.

Strategies can come from many different sources and it is wise to consider all possible ways of generating potential strategies. Some strategies may seem to follow logically and obviously from the objectives, but others may evolve in a flash of inspiration. When the list of alternative strategies has been prepared, they should be evaluated to determine which will best satisfy the objectives. You should also determine which strategies can be best implemented with the resources and capabilities that your company has.

Strategies should be listed under the headings of the four main elements of the marketing mix – product, pricing, promotion and distribution. Examples of specific marketing strategies for these major functions are shown below together with some of the tactics that could be employed.

Products

Strategy – change product portfolio/mix
   Tactics:

- Offer only one product line.
- Expand your product line to cover a wider market.
- Develop separate products for different markets.
- Make different versions of the product with different names for different markets.
- Acquire new products that complement existing products through the acquisition of new companies.

Strategy – drop, add or modify products
   Tactics:

- Drop marginal products.
- Develop new products to supersede old products.
- Launch modified product.

Strategy – change design, quality or performance
   Tactics:

- Establish a quality image through the development of quality products.
- Distinguish your product from your competitor's product in the eyes of your customers.
- Establish a reputation for innovation.
- Create new uses for your existing product by improving performance or by adding exclusive features.

Strategy – consolidate/standardize the product
   Tactics:

- Rationalize your product line.
- Drop expensive extras/specials.

Pricing

Strategy – change price, terms or conditions for particular product groups in particular market segments
   Tactics:

- Set price at 10 per cent below market leader.
- Devise strategy to meet specific pricing policies of competitors.
- Reduce price of product to maximize sales (to allow increased production and reduce unit production cost).
- Price product low and obtain maximum profit on spare parts.
- Price product high and use low mark-up on spare parts.

Strategy – skimming policy
Tactics:

- Set price of new product at a level 30 per cent above previous products.
- Sell on new revolutionary design features and benefits.
- Be prepared to reduce price as volume increases if competitors enter market.

Strategy – penetration policy
Tactics:

- Set low price for new product to discourage competitors from entering market.
- Increase turnover to level where product becomes profitable at this price level.

Strategy – discount policies
Tactics:

- Offer quantity discount to encourage larger unit purchases.
- Offer discount to encourage online purchasing.
- Offer retrospective discount based on level of purchases this year.
- Offer discount level for next year based on level of purchases this year.

Promotion

Examples of strategies and tactics relating to personal selling, advertising and sales promotion are shown below.
Strategy – improve sales force performance
Tactics:

- Recruit new sales manager.
- Carry out advanced sales training.

- Introduce new appraisal scheme.
- Change sales force incentive scheme.

Strategy – change advertising
   Tactics:

- Increase advertising for the product in specific markets.
- Start new advertising campaign.
- Carry out e-mailshot.
- Update and expand website.
- Add 'web analytics' for e-marketing.
- Increase company image advertising.

Strategy – increase sales promotion
   Tactics:

- Offer limited time promotion with chance for participants to win prizes.
- Introduce voucher scheme to encourage repeat purchase.
- Offer incentive scheme to distributors.

Strategy – increase online advertising and sales promotion
   Tactics:

- Update and expand website.
- Use e-mailshots.
- Advertise on industry-specific websites.
- Take space on sites such as www.yell.com and gb.kompass. co. uk.

Strategy – increase use of social media
   Tactics:

- Use social media consultant to plan campaign.
- Set up company blog with RSS update feature.

- Set up company Facebook page.
- Create company Twitter account.

Examples of strategies and tactics involving exhibitions are shown below:

Strategy – increase exhibition coverage
    Tactics:

- Increase attendance and stand size at major industry exhibitions.
- Set up webinars for major industry exhibitions.
- Use government assistance for overseas exhibitions.
- Encourage overseas distributors to exhibit more and supply equipment and personnel as support.

Strategy – introduce new product
    Tactics:

- Carry out high key product launch.
- Support product launch with advertising campaign.
- Support product launch by exhibiting at major exhibitions.

Distribution (place)

Distribution involves marketing channels, physical distribution and customer service.

Strategy – change channels
    Tactics:

- Set up own distribution direct to stores.
- Change distributor for area.
- Increase own sales coverage.
- Expand online shop.
- Increase number of warehouses for product.
- Reduce to use of only one large warehouse.

Strategy – improve distributor performance
   Tactics:

- Implement programme of distributor support visits.
- Set up quarterly distributor Zoom meetings.
- Set up annual distributor conferences.
- Set up targeted incentive scheme.
- Agree joint advertising campaigns with key distributors.

Strategy – improve service
   Tactics:

- Set up national service network.
- Arrange service through major company with service centres throughout the area.

Strategy – improve service to key accounts
   Tactics:

- Set up key account management system.
- Appoint key account management group.
- Plan programme of customer meetings and follow-up programme.

We will now consider the strategies that The Equipment Manufacturing Company intends to adopt in order to achieve the objectives of its UK marketing plan.

In the scope of the UK plan they intend to concentrate mainly on expanding their existing markets with their existing products. They will also expand the sales of the new product packages into existing markets. These are low risk strategies. They accept the need for new products and product improvements, but more work needs to be carried out to identify what is required. The main products to be considered are the ball valves and the 'type S' filters. They will carry out customer/competitor surveys over the next six months to define the market requirements for the new products. The products will then be developed. Since this will take at least 18 months, it is intended that the UK marketing plan will be revised in 12 months' time when the situation is clearer. The UK marketing plan will concentrate on areas of organization and sales coverage that clearly need attention and the strategies being adopted are mainly *developing and attacking* strategies.

The key strategies for The Equipment Manufacturing Company for its UK plan are listed below:

- Products
  - package products (ball valves with filters);
  - design new ball valve;
  - design replacement for 'type S' filters.
- Pricing
  - additional discount will be offered for online purchases to encourage use of our online shop;
  - penetration policy will be adopted with packages since these will help us to sell more valves;
  - penetration policy will be adopted on 'type K' filters since these generate a large proportion of replacement cartridges.
- Promotion
  - change salesforce organization;
  - recruit additional sales personnel;
  - restructure sales management;
  - increase advertising;
  - increase exhibition coverage;
  - use e-mailshots;
  - update and expand website;
  - add 'web analytics' for e-marketing.
- Distribution
  - change distribution;
  - appoint distributor sales manager;
  - increase own sales coverage;
  - expand online shop.

Exercise

Now prepare some preliminary strategies for your marketing plan.

Our preliminary strategies are:

Products

_____

_____

_____

_____

Price

_____

_____

_____

_____

Promotion

_____

_____

_____

_____

Distribution

_____

_____

_____

_____

Action plans

Top tip

Once you have selected the outline strategies and tactics to achieve your marketing objectives, you need to turn these strategies into programmes or action plans that will enable you to give clear instructions to your staff.

Each action plan should include:

- current position – where you are now;
- aims – what to do/where do you want to go;
- action – what you need to do to get there;
- person responsible – who will do it;
- start date;
- finish date;
- budgeted cost.

Each action plan would need to be broken down into its component parts. Table 4.1 shows a suggested layout for an action plan for The Equipment Manufacturing Company.

Table 4.1   Presentation of an action plan

Action plan e-mailshot – filter packages						
Department: Sales						
Aim	Current position	Action	By	Start	Finish	Cost
Carry out e-mailshot	Need 'opt in' email list of target companies	Purchase list	ALT	9.1.X6	16.1.X6	£200
	Need material for website	Prepare material for website	JDT	9.1.X6	20.2.X6	£300
	Need link to website	Create link on email	JDT	21.2.X6	21.2.X6	£10
		Send out	ILH	27.2.X6	27.2.X6	£100

This plan is to carry out the strategy of 'carry out an e-mailshot'. The e-mailshot is for filter packages aimed at the water-treatment industry.

Each of the actions on this action plan could be broken down into a number of parts. In the preparation of the material for the website there would be a number of stages, including:

- liaising with the production department on when a completed filter package will be available;

- having the filter package photographed;

- liaising with the engineering department to prepare technical information to include in the web page text;

- writing the text;

- preparing preliminary layout of text and images on the test web page;

- proofreading the test web page and checking the web links;
- publishing the web page live.

After scheduling your activities on the basis of action plans you should combine the individual action plans and programmes into larger functional programmes (product, pricing, promotion, distribution). These functional programmes would appear in the marketing plan. They would then be developed into an overall schedule – a master programme that can be used for controlling the implementation of the plan. This is the schedule of what/where/how in the written plan. Although it would only be the larger functional programmes and the master programme schedule that would appear in the written plan, each of the smaller plans and programmes would need to be communicated to those who have to carry them out.

Summary points

Marketing strategies are the methods by which you achieve your marketing objectives.

- They relate to *products, pricing, advertising/promotion* and *distribution.*

- You should select those that will best satisfy your objectives and which can be effectively implemented using the resources and capabilities that you have available.

- In order that they may be carried out, strategies must be converted into programmes or action plans.

05
The distribution plan

Before you can plan your advertising and sales promotion you need to select the right channels for your product and your business from those available. This is part of the distribution plan, which will always be part of any marketing plan.

The physical distribution of goods is only one aspect of distribution as defined by marketing planners.

Top tip

Distribution involves:

- Marketing channels.
- Physical distribution.
- Customer service.

Marketing channels

Marketing channels are the means that a company can select to get into contact with its potential customers. If its potential customers are unaware of the product, they will not buy it. There are a wide variety of different channels that a company can use. Figure 5.1 shows a typical selection of available marketing channels.

Figure 5.1 Marketing channels

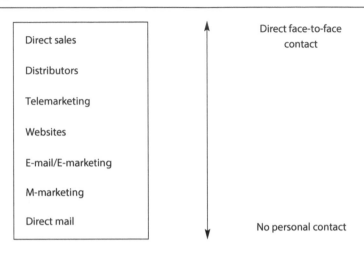

Direct sales is an expensive channel to operate and is mainly restricted to high value industrial goods. The bulk of advertising expenditure is used on consumer goods, particularly low value, repeat buy items such as food and household consumables. Consumer goods are usually sold through distributors, wholesalers and retailers rather than through direct selling, but it is usually still necessary for the company to have a salesforce to sell to these distributors, wholesalers and retailers.

The characteristics of the product you are selling will have a considerable influence on the mix of marketing channels that you finally select (see Figure 5.2). The number of levels of channels of distribution will also affect prices because of the level of discounts that will need to be built into the price structure.

Figure 5.2 The influence of product characteristics on distribution channels

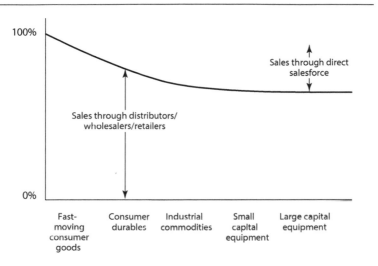

Direct sales

In a perfect world direct selling with the salesperson face to face with the customer would give a company the maximum possibility of getting the message across and closing the sale. In the real world this is just not cost effective and all companies employ a mixture of direct and indirect sales techniques.

The advantages of personal selling are:

- it allows two-way communication between the buyer and seller;
- the salesperson can tailor the presentation to the individual needs of the customer;
- the salesperson comes to know and be known by the customers;
- the salesperson can negotiate directly on price, delivery and discounts;
- the salesperson can close the sale;
- the salesperson can monitor customer satisfaction levels.

Distribution

Distribution channels for consumer goods

In consumer goods industries distributors could be retailers, wholesalers or even companies that sell to wholesalers. In consumer markets it is usually the manufacturer who carries out the advertising campaigns to make the customer aware of the product. This is often the only way that the manufacturer can get his product message over to the consumer. The wholesale/retail system means that the manufacturer can deal with a smaller number of accounts and make larger individual deliveries of products. Because wholesalers and retailers hold stock this reduces the manufacturer's requirement to hold stock. He also uses their knowledge of the market and customer contacts. The manufacturer gives the wholesaler a trade discount which is usually substantial because it has to cover the wholesaler's costs of stocking, buying in bulk, redistributing to retailers or end users and, of course, his profit.

The distribution channels available for consumer goods are shown in Figure 5.3.

Distribution channels for services

For services the situation is different. There is no product on the shelf and so there is no requirement for wholesalers and retailers. The company supplying the service may sell it direct to the end-user or through an intermediary. The intermediary could be a commission agent, such as a travel agent or accommodation bureau, or a franchise-holder in the case of businesses offering onsite windscreen replacement, car scratch repair or many of the fast food chains.

Figure 5.4 shows distribution channels for services.

Figure 5.3 Distribution channels for consumer goods

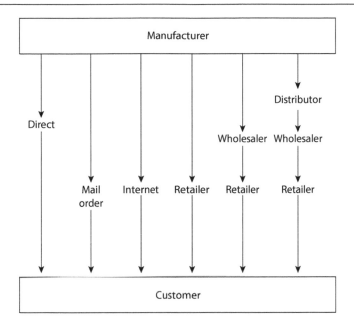

Figure 5.4 Distribution channels for services

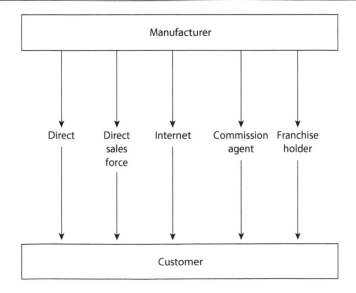

Distribution channels for industrial goods

For industrial goods it is not usual to use wholesale/retail outlets like those used for consumer goods. Direct sales to customers generally make up a larger proportion of sales than with consumer goods, but the use of commission agents and distributors is widespread. The most common distinction is that a distributor holds stock and an agent or rep does not. Figure 5.5 shows distribution channels for industrial goods.

Figure 5.5　Distribution channels for industrial goods

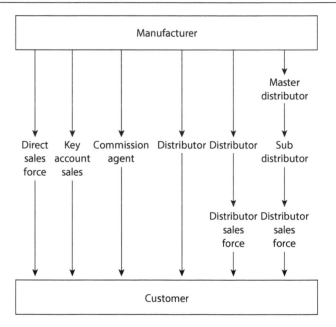

Most industrial manufacturers have a direct sales force. With industrial goods there will often be 'key accounts' who are serviced differently from smaller customers. Commission agents act on behalf of a number of manufacturers of different but related products. The order is normally placed on the manufacturer by the customer and a commission is paid to the agent. A distributor takes over the selling role of the manufacturer and most distributors will have their own sales force dealing with customers. A distributor would normally be expected to hold enough stock to service the geographical area for which he is responsible. He may be an exclusive or a non-exclusive distributor.

A direct sales force can be structured:

- by product;
- by area;
- by industry;
- by account.

Distributors can also be appointed on the same basis.

Managing distributors

Day-to-day management

A good distributor will have a number of key product ranges – often as many as six. Ideally, you want to be sure that your product range is one of their top product ranges, but you have to accept that the same sales people who sell your product range will be putting in time selling other company's products. If you try to support the business from your office with just phone calls and emails, you should not be surprised to find that other company's products are getting more sales time.

Top tip

To manage a distributor properly you need to visit them regularly, both to review progress and to give support where needed.

Promotional and presentation material

You will need to provide your distributors with an adequate supply of sales material such as leaflets, data sheets and presentations. If you supply most of the material as pdf files, they can print off copies when they need them and have them available on their websites for customers to download.

Your overseas distributors will need to produce some of your sales materials and presentations in their own language. You need to make the files containing the key sales leaflets and data sheets available to the distributor, so that they can use either their own qualified staff or a local agency to produce versions of these in their own language. Key PowerPoint presentations can also be sent to them for translation.

If you are going to carry out training of your distributor's sales team, the material you will be using needs to be sent out to the distributor for translation prior to the training.

Distributor meetings or conferences

A distributor conference is similar to a sales conference, but involves a company's distribution (either domestic, overseas or both). The emphasis is on sales and growing them. The delegates would normally be the key sales and management personnel from a company's major distributors. Distributor conferences are often organized to take place in the spring or early summer – before the holiday season starts. The results and agreed targets resulting from the conference can then be fed into your company budgeting process in the autumn.

Improving distributor performance

Making regular support visits and having regular distributor meetings will motivate your distributors. But to improve their performance, you need to work with them and agree specific targets. Obviously, you will agree annual sales targets with them, but you should also set other goals. These could include:

- sales targets by sub-area or by industry;
- targeting a list of specific key accounts;
- targeting a new industry (for them).

If they are going to work on this type of target they will expect additional support from you. This could involve:

- setting up a targeted incentive scheme – either for the distributor or for the members of their sales team;
- jointly funding targeted advertising campaigns;
- support for a particular exhibition in the form of technical sales support, providing exhibition equipment or even part-funding of stand and other costs.

Telemarketing

Telemarketing involves selling and marketing by telephone rather than by direct physical contact. Generally, it has been found that telemarketing is most effective when it supplements the field sales-force activity rather than completely replacing it. It is cost effective because 40–50 telephone calls can be made per day whereas 6–10 personal visits per day is normal for direct sales calls. The main advantages of telemarketing are:

- lower cost than direct salesforce;
- it frees up the salesperson's time by reducing routine calling activity;
- it increases frequency of customer contact;
- it allows dormant accounts to be revived;
- in some cases it can be farmed out to a professional telemarketing company.

The types of telemarketing services available have expanded greatly in recent years. There are now a wide range of companies specializing in business to business (B2B) and business to customer (B2C) telemarketing. Services offered include:

- Lead generation.
- Database maintenance.
- Data collection.
- Customer relations.
- Prospecting.
- Sales.
- Customer retention.

Telemarketing uses a mix of telephone landlines and mobile phones. This will gradually change over the next decade. Before 2010, virtually all telephone users had a landline, even though the use of mobile phones was widespread. By 2020 about 22 per cent of households in the United Kingdom and more than 60 per cent of households in the United States had no landline and only a mobile phone. Analysts estimate that by 2025 the majority of households in the UK will have only mobile phones and that by 2030 only a small percentage of people in either the UK or the US will still have a landline.

Taking your business online

The internet provides companies with a major sales channel for all types of products. Online purchasing is continuing to grow at an amazing rate. In the UK online retail sales grew by 6.7 per cent in 2019. According to eMarketer, the coronavirus pandemic accelerated the trend dramatically and online retail sales in the UK increased from 21.8 per cent of total sales in 2019 to 32 per cent in 2020. In 2021 they fell back slightly to about 30 per cent of the total, but are still predicted to continue to grow in the coming years. The situation was similar in the United States where analysis of US Department of Commerce data by Digital Commerce 360 showed that online retail sales increased from 14.3 per cent of the total in 2018 to 19.6 per cent in 2020.

The impact of the internet on prices

It has long been said that the two main effects of the internet on businesses are to drive down prices and to force uncompetitive companies out of business. The reality is not quite so clear cut. With regard to prices, the internet works more as a mechanism that reduces the cost of getting information about products and prices. A customer who wants to buy an electrical item no longer has to visit several local shops to compare prices. He can find out the average and lowest price of the item online. He can buy it online or, if he wants to view the item, he can still go into his local electrical superstore. If it is much more expensive he can still opt to buy online. Research shows that 81 per cent of internet users research products online before making a purchase (either in-store or online). So the main effect of the internet is to make it more difficult for retailers to sell overpriced goods and to lead to a lower variation in prices and through that a lower level of price.

Top tip

A study by economists at the University of Chicago looked at the impact of e-commerce on three industries: bookshops, travel agencies and new-car dealerships. It concluded that in all three cases the growth of online shopping didn't just affect prices, it also changed the structure of the industry. As you might expect, the main change was that larger companies grew and some small ones went out of business. But the study also suggests that although people who want lower prices will go to the larger companies, small companies in the same industry can grow if they meet a specific need or offer a particular service or benefit.

Ordinary website or e-commerce site?

So should you take your business online? I think it is clear that all companies need a website. But it is easier to sell your products online if they are easy to store, pack and dispatch. If Amazon gets a glut of orders, they can just ship some of the goods a few days later. Companies selling perishable goods such as online grocery firms cannot do that – and their customers want what they have ordered when they need it.

So you need a website and your website needs to be well constructed and easy to navigate so that customers will use it and will come back to it. Any website will be a channel to market, because it will pass information to your customers in the same way that direct sales or telemarketing can. But not all companies need to take orders on their website and not every company needs to have a true e-commerce site. Particularly in service industries, it may be necessary to provide individual quotations for individual jobs or projects. The details of the enquiry can be taken on the website through the 'contact us' page, but a separate quotation would then need to be prepared and emailed to the customer.

Email/e-marketing

E-marketing and web analytics have brought about big changes in marketing tactics. Email is the perfect vehicle to build lifetime relationships with customers. There are a large number of e-marketing companies that can supply permission-based technology to help businesses communicate, and build or add to their existing database of potential and existing customers, creating targeted direct e-marketing campaigns with information and offerings specific to each customer's interests. Permission marketing can turn online visitors into lifetime customers by allowing regular communication with both existing and prospective customers. Giving consumers total control of the messages they receive is the future of direct marketing on the internet. Permission marketing is the ideal solution to personalize relationships and secure continued customer support.

With opt-in email, responses (5 to 15 per cent) are far greater than those from banner advertising (0.5 per cent), or traditional direct mail (1 to 3 per cent). In addition to a greater response rate, a direct email marketing campaign is only a fraction of the cost of more traditional methods of marketing.

Email bulletins can even track how many users open the emails and what, if anything, they click on in the bulletin. This is far more effective at collating customer information than direct mail.

If you are new to email marketing it is sensible to consult a professional email marketing company to help you plan your campaign. They will be able to provide you with opt-in email lists that are relevant to your business and will also be able to help you to set up and manage your email campaign. Once the campaign is under way, they will also be able to provide you with analysis and data reporting.

M-commerce

Mobile commerce (m-commerce) is a type of e-commerce conducted through mobile devices such as mobile phones, personal digital assistants and other mobile devices with a wireless connection – including smartphones (iPhones, Android phones, etc), tablets (iPad, Kindle, etc), netbooks and notebooks. As well as bringing new opportunities for selling online, m-commerce allows you to use mobile marketing to interact with your customers whilst on the move.

> **Top tip**
>
> The four main marketing tools for m-commerce are:
> - mobile web;
> - mobile applications or 'apps';
> - mobile advertising;
> - SMS or MMS messages.

M-commerce is expanding at a tremendous rate. Ofcom figures show that by 2020 95 per cent of adults in the UK owned a mobile phone and 82 per cent owned a smartphone. (Sixty per cent of people in the UK used their mobile handsets to access the internet.) The ownership of smartphones continues to increase rapidly. In 2016 2.1 billion people worldwide were using smartphones, but by 2021 this had increased to 3.8 billion. More than 50 per cent of all online orders in the UK are now being placed using a mobile device (a smartphone or tablet computer) and in 2020 over 50 per cent of internet users in the US used their mobile phones to purchase products online.

Direct mail

Direct mail includes mail-order business and the use of mailshots. Mailshots involve sending information on a specific product by mail to potential customers on a mailing list. They rely on the accuracy of the mailing list used, and a low return rate (1 to 3 per cent) is considered quite normal. Marketing List Limited, https://marketinglists.co.uk, is one of the UK's largest suppliers of business and consumer mailing lists. They have a UK business database with over three million records and can provide mailing lists targeted by company size, industry, SIC code, area and a number of other criteria. Their consumer information is even more extensive with a comprehensive list of 37 million consumers with profiled information. They can provide custom built mailing lists using over 300 different profiles, which can include wealth, housing type, rateable value and general lifestyle factors.

Mailshots are still very popular because small items or samples can be sent with the mailshot – something that is not possible with email. But in many cases they are being superseded by e-mailshots on the grounds of cost and efficiency.

Physical distribution, warehousing and factory location

Physical distribution involves not only the holding of stock, but also communicating within the distribution network and the way that the product is packaged for distribution. The proximity of the factory to its markets is more important with high-bulk–low-value goods than with sophisticated capital goods, but stocking at the factory, at warehouses or logistics centres is an important part of distribution strategy that will determine whether you can give as good a service as your competitors – or better.

Customer service

For the distribution plan we are only interested in the aspects of customer service that affect distribution. This really relates to the level of availability of the product to the customer. Distribution is about getting the product to the right place (for the customer) at the right time. Theoretically you want to offer your customers 100 per cent availability of the product. In practice this is not possible. It is necessary to find a balance between the costs and benefits involved. The costs of extra availability cannot exceed the extra revenue that will be gained as a result.

Example

Below we consider the *marketing channels* and *physical distribution* used by The Equipment Manufacturing Company in the UK.

Marketing channels

The Equipment Manufacturing Company uses a mixture of direct sales (to large key accounts and contracting companies) and distributors (who hold stock of valves/filters and spares). It has recently started to use telemarketing to follow up dormant accounts. It has also set up an online shop on its website.

Physical distribution

The company manufactures valves at its factory in Manchester and filters at its factory in the South of England and holds a stock of components and spare parts at the factory. It does not stock finished valves or filters and only supplies to order. The company's distributors operate on a discount level of 30 per cent from the company's list price and this finances the equipment that they hold in stock. The company uses local haulage contractors for deliveries of finished goods. More urgent deliveries are made using nationwide overnight services such as DHL, UPS and TNT. The company operates an MRP (Materials Resource Planning) system with a computer database that includes order processing and invoicing. In addition the company operates a computer database for its distribution network and can advise one distributor where he can find a component (with another distributor) if he does not have it in stock. With the agreement of their distributors, the company is making this database accessible to all distributors via its website (this part of the website will be restricted and will only be accessible to authorized company and distributor personnel who will have to log in individually).

Exercise

Now consider the marketing channels and distribution used by your own company for the products and areas covered by your marketing plan. Detail these below:

Marketing channels

_____

_____

_____

Physical distribution/logistics

_____

_____

_____

In the distribution plan it is necessary to consider if a change in marketing channels or physical distribution is necessary. For The Equipment Manufacturing Company sales of valves are concentrated in the Midlands and the North of England – where the company's distribution is strong. Its sales in Wales, Scotland and Northern Ireland are minimal. The distributors in these areas should be evaluated and possibly replaced. It may also be worthwhile considering acquiring one or more distributors to give the company its own logistics base in a particular area.

Summary points

You need to be sure that you are using the best mix of the available marketing channels to sell your product. These could include:

- direct sales;
- distributors/retailers/wholesalers;
- telemarketing;
- direct mail;
- the internet;
- email/e-marketing;
- m-commerce.

The characteristics of the product will influence the mix of marketing channels used.

06

The advertising and promotions plan

The advertising and promotions plan involves personnel, advertising and promotions.

Personnel

Once you have selected your mix of distribution channels you can decide on the personnel requirements of the plan. As shown in Figure 5.2, your product will determine to some extent the channels that you use. The channels will determine to some extent the type of sales organization that you need. In the situation analysis we carried out a SWOT analysis for the sales organization of The Equipment Manufacturing Company (Figure 2.5). This indicated the weaknesses that need to be addressed and the opportunities that we can take. We now need to detail the existing sales structure and the proposed structure for the plan. In doing this we need to indicate which personnel are existing and which are additional (or replacements!).

The existing UK sales organization of The Equipment Manufacturing Company is shown in Figure 6.1.

Figure 6.1   Existing sales organization

With this structure, the sales engineers are selling to large key accounts and contracting companies and the UK sales manager is running the salesforce and distribution. The industry specialists are sales engineers who have both area and industry responsibilities. This structure lacks focus. There are a number of different ways that it could be restructured to improve focus. My proposal is shown in Figure 6.2.

Figure 6.2   Proposed new sales organization

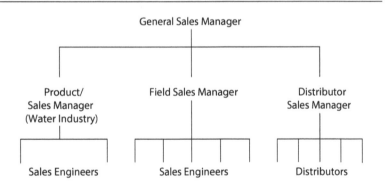

In this structure, the general sales manager and distributor sales manager are new personnel who need to be recruited. The UK sales manager has become the field sales manager. Field sales is the job he does best. The sales engineer who is the expert in the water industry becomes the product/sales manager for the water industry and a separate salesforce is being created to develop water industry sales. The list of new and existing sales personnel is shown in Figure 6.3.

Figure 6.3 New and existing sales personnel

Position	Existing personnel	New personnel	Total
General sales mgr		1	1
UK sales mgr	1		
Field sales mgr			1
Distributor sales mgr		1	1
Water industry mgr			1
Sales engineers	6	1	6
Total	7	3	10

Exercise

Now consider the sales organization for your plan. Draw up the existing organization structure, detail its strengths and weaknesses, analyse the focus that you have and the focus that you need. Draw up your new structure and if it is different from the existing structure note the new personnel required.

_____

_____

_____

_____

_____

Advertising and promotions

Top tip

The purpose of advertising is to get a message across to the customer. Advertising operates at three levels:

- it informs;
- it persuades;
- it reinforces.

Advertising to inform normally relates to the promotion of new products and services. Advertising to persuade is what most people understand as advertising. There is also the public relations side of advertising – promotional public relations. This includes media relations and exhibitions.

Because advertising on television and in the national press is very expensive, most television and national press advertising relates to consumer goods with large annual sales or services such as banking and insurance. The advertising of industrial and capital goods uses much narrower and more specific outlets such as industry-specific magazines or websites. Repeat advertising is more effective than one-off advertisements. The same advert repeated every week or every month in a limited number of outlets is more effective than different one-off adverts in a wide range of outlets.

Similarly, industrial products are normally exhibited at exhibitions that are specific for that industry rather than general trade fairs. Most industrial companies now also use their website to provide information on their products and to publicize new products and sales successes. The advantage of a website is that even small companies can give the impression of being large and knowledgeable.

In addition to company websites, there is now also a range of independent websites for specific types of industrial equipment (pumps and valves, vacuum equipment, mixing equipment) or industries (pulp and paper, chemical manufacturing, water and waste treatment).

Advertising online

If you want to do any advertising online, you need to have a website. Most online advertising (search advertising) is geared to directing people to your website. According to *Adweek*, 81 per cent of US shoppers conduct online research before they make a purchase. 60 per cent begin by using a search engine to find the products they want, and 61 per cent will read product reviews before making any purchase. Your website is a permanent shop window that is available 24 hours a day 7 days a week.

As early as 2009 the UK became the first major economy where advertisers spent more on digital advertising than on television advertising. This was swiftly followed by other countries and according to eMarketer, digital advertising spending in the Unites States overtook spending on television advertising for the first time in 2016. In 2019 digital advertising globally accounted for 50 per cent of the total advertising spend and television advertising for only 27 per cent. By 2019 digital advertising accounted for 56 per cent of the total UK advertising spend compared with only 19 per cent for television advertising. The figures for the US were 47 per cent for digital advertising compared with only 27 per cent for television.

Figures from the Advertising Association show that in 2019 56 per cent of total digital advertising spending in the UK was on search advertising on websites such as Google and 44 per cent on online display-related advertising such as banners on websites, rich media, digital video and sponsorship. In terms of format, mobile advertising accounted for about two-thirds of all digital advertising.

Advertising on social media websites

Social media websites such as Facebook and YouTube are trying to increase their advertising revenues. Both provide full details of advertising possibilities on their websites. Facebook allows you to select your audience by location, age and interests and to test out simple image and text-based ads. They suggest that companies advertising on Facebook can advertise their own webpage, create demand for their products by creating relevant adverts or publicize an event such as a product launch or company anniversary. Payment is either by 'pay per click' or by 'impression' (visitors see the add, whether they click on it or not). You can set a daily budget, which can be adjusted up or down at any time.

Banners and display advertising

Display 'banners' or banner ads were the first major method used for online advertising and 10 years ago they had the bulk of the market. But in recent years this has dropped to only about 20 per cent of internet advertising as 'pay per click' or 'keyword' advertising has become the predominant force and other display-related advertising formats such as rich media and digital video have also taken market share. Banner ads are small adverts that normally come in various rectangular forms. They appear on websites and serve as a link directly to the advertiser's website. When you click on the banner your browser instantly redirects you to the advertiser's website. The popularity of banner ads is in part due to the fact that they are simple to produce and publish. They are also highly measurable. Depending on the ad and the product or service, advertisers can calculate the cost per sale – this is the amount of advertising money that is spent to make one sale.

Pay per click (PPC) or keyword advertising

Search engines and many websites (including social networking sites such as Facebook) carry small adverts with embedded URLs.

When someone clicks on these adverts, the company that put them there is charged. This is now the preferred method of online advertising and has been growing at a remarkable rate. Unlike traditional advertising, pay per click is user activated. Users like it, because it costs them nothing and they only use it if there is something that attracts them. The advantage of pay per click for advertisers is that they only pay for the actual click through to their site. With other methods of advertising, both on and offline, you have no guarantee as to how much you may have to pay to attract each visitor. It is a fact that visitors who click through to your site through a search engine are quite likely to purchase products, because these visitors are actively looking for the type of product that you are offering.

When you set up a PPC advertising campaign, you can usually set a maximum amount of spend per day or a total overall spend for your campaign, so that you know what your maximum spend could be.

The most popular service is Google Adwords. Google can deliver more from PPC than smaller search engines because they have the largest number of users of any search engine. Google try to make it very easy for companies to use their Adwords service – they will even help you create a website if you don't have one. Adwords is a keyword-based product and Google say that all you have to do is:

- create your ad;
- choose your keywords;
- set the limit of your geographical coverage;
- set your budget.

So PPC advertising is very targeted – at a consumer looking for something that is quite specific. You can limit it to specific geographical regions to avoid paying for 'interest' clicks that are not likely to result in business. You only pay when someone clicks on your advert, but that means that your advert has to appear. You can improve the likelihood of that happening by bidding for keywords.

Even though setting up and operating PPC advertising is quite straightforward, it can be time consuming and complicated to manage properly. Many companies therefore decide to pay an expert to manage this service for them to make sure that they get the most out of their PPC advertising.

Search engine optimization (SEO)

The huge increase in the number of companies operating and selling on the internet has dramatically increased the competition between companies to get visitors to their websites rather than to those of their competitors. When carrying out a web search, most people will only look at the first page of search results and often only at the top two or three results. So making sure that your site gets high up in the results is important to the success of your website. There are ways of improving your search engine ranking and search engine optimization is the method of achieving this. Search engine optimization is a complex science and there is a lot of jargon that is difficult to understand. So it is better to use a specialist SEO company. Using an SEO company can be a one off cost for an initial optimization or an ongoing consultancy.

The increasing use of PR

Top tip

Public relations is an important part of marketing and apart from its main objective of creating and maintaining goodwill for an organization, it can be used to great effect to enhance advertising, sales promotion – even exhibitions and conferences.

No business can be successful without the effective use of public relations. Although large companies may have their own PR departments, most companies prefer to use the services of a public relations consultancy or a marketing agency/consultancy that also handles public relations work.

Advertising vs PR?

Even in the recession of 2009, spending on public relations in the US grew by more than 3 per cent, whereas in the same year spending on advertising fell by 8 per cent. One of the reasons that PR does so well is because a PR campaign is often cheaper than mass advertising and its impact, in terms of coverage in the media or online, can be measured more easily. Taking a full page colour advertisement in one of the main Sunday newspapers can cost a multinational company as much as £100,000. Getting the company mentioned in an article could cost a few thousand pounds or even less in a small targeted PR campaign. This is why so many companies cut the advertising budget but retain PR – it's much cheaper and much more trusted. The trust issue is also key. People trust the news media so an article mentioning the benefits of a product is trusted far more than an advertisement, often at a fraction of the cost too.

Developing your social media strategy

Top tip

Using social media as a PR channel for your company is a fairly straightforward concept. The beauty is that it is just as easy (if not easier) for a small company to do as for a large multinational corporation.

A small company is likely to react to comments on their user blog and answer messages on their Facebook account more quickly than a large corporation might do and this is important. To get started, the types of things you need to do are to set up your own blog on your website, create a presence on Facebook and create a Twitter account. It is not as easy as it sounds.

When you decide that you want to take your PR online, I would recommend the following:

- Take advice from a consultancy to help you develop a social media strategy. Bear in mind that you may need to develop several strategies, each tailored to a different social media channel.

- Make sure that you have an adequate and ongoing dedicated resource to manage your social media programme. (This may need to be a dedicated person.) Once you have set up the sites, you need to continue to put material on them regularly and to respond to any criticisms within 24 hours.

Once you are up and running, remember that to be successful you need to properly interact with your customers. Don't put information on your blog just because it interests you. Listen to what people have to say. Don't ignore criticism – respond, and respond quickly. This is another thing that PR consultants can help you with. They can track what your customers are saying about you online and respond directly to any negative commentary that is building up.

How does it work in practice?

Twitter can be a much more effective way of making a complaint than phoning a customer service number. Experience shows that companies respond much more quickly and efficiently when people tweet their complaints. Companies as diverse as Chrysler and Best Buy now employ 'Twitter teams' to reply to whinging tweets. Most airports and airlines are now attempting to use some form of direct Twitter communication. London Gatwick Airport uses its Twitter feed @Gatwick_Airport to publish updates about the airport and to encourage direct feedback.

The Department for International Trade (DIT) makes extensive use of digital channels. Its export home page at www.great.gov.uk provides access to DIT services including business opportunities, events, country and sector information. You can set alerts for business opportunities and events, as well as for updates to the DIT website and blog. The Department's use of social media on Facebook, LinkedIn and Twitter also allows you to join a community of exporters from across the UK, exchanging experiences and advice with the aim of inspiring, engaging and supporting a new generation of exporters and cultivating a national exporting movement.

A DIT spokesperson said: 'At the Department for International Trade we use digital channels to promote our activities to a wide business audience, be they those who have not done business overseas before or existing exporters looking for new opportunities. We've found our channels really useful in raising awareness and driving traffic to our services. But we don't just use our channels for pushing messages out. It's also about engaging with and understanding our audience so we can help them succeed in growing their business internationally'.

You can get a lot out of using social media if you are prepared to make the investment and then work at it. But it is not something that you can start off and then expect to run by itself.

The Equipment Manufacturing Company is targeting the water industry. Table 6.1 and Figure 6.4 show a press advertising schedule and exhibition cost schedule it has prepared.

The advertising schedule includes the annual cost of subscribing to the website www.waterproducts.com. This is a website that specializes in products used in the water and waste treatment

Table 6.1   Advertising schedule

		Rate per insertion	Total cost												
Advertising															
Application: Water industry										**Year: 20X6**					
Media	**No**	**£**	**£**	J	F	M	A	M	J	J	A	S	O	N	D
Water and Waste Treatment	2	1,800	3,600					X				X			
Water Services	2	1,500	3,000						X				X		
Water Bulletin	3	800	2,400			X			X			X			
Water products.com	1	2,000	2,000	X	X	X	X	X	X	X	X	X	X	X	X
Total cost			11,000												

Figure 6.4   Schedule of expenditure for a major exhibition

Exhibition costs	
Name of exhibition: IWEX Location: NEC Birmingham Date: 6th–8th November 20X6 Stand size: 64 m² (8 m × 8 m) Stand Contractor: Exhibition Contractors Ltd	
Costs	£
Stand space rental	8,000
Design, supply and build	10,000
Artwork, photographic panels	5,000
Rental of carpets, furniture, lights, phone, etc	3,000
Hotel bills/expenditure for stand staff	2,000
Total	28,000

industries. Descriptions of their individual products for the water industry are shown on the site and pdf files of their technical literature and datasheets can be downloaded from it. The site has a 'web analytics' system and can provide the company with lists of users who visit the site and details of which of the company's products they have looked at. The company will also be carrying out some targeted mail/e-mailshots and expanding its website to include 'web analytics' for e-marketing. The costs of these items will go into the advertising and promotions plan.

Exercise

Prepare similar schedules and costs for promotions that you intend to include in your plan.

_____

_____

_____

Summary points

The advertising and promotions plan involves personnel, advertising and sales promotion.

- The purpose of advertising is to get a message across to the customer.

- Public relations (PR) is increasingly being used to enhance both advertising and sales promotion.

- Advertising on social media websites should only be undertaken as part of a coordinated social media strategy.

- You should include the details, schedules and costs of the advertising and sales promotion campaigns that are included in your marketing plan.

07
Costs and budgets

In carrying out the marketing planning process and preparing your plan, you have already seen how to decide on strategies and to prepare the action plans to enable you to carry out your strategies and achieve your objectives. You have seen how realistic objectives can be set. But what about your strategies and action plans? They may be feasible, but are they cost-effective? If the cost of implementing your strategies and carrying out your action plans is greater than the contribution to company profits resulting from the additional sales forecast in the plan, you might as well forget the plan now – unless you can devise other strategies to achieve the same objectives.

Top tip

How can you decide if your marketing plan is viable? Only by preparing a partial profit and loss account. For sales personnel, this can be the most difficult part of the whole process. All companies have a particular way that they put together the financial data that goes into their profit and loss account. It is wise to involve someone from your finance and accounting department to help you to prepare the partial profit and loss account that you need for your plan.

Profit and loss account

The profit and loss account is a summary of the success or failure of the transactions of a company over a period of time. It lists income generated and costs incurred. From the point of view of our marketing plan, we are not interested in anything below the line of operating profit, because our marketing activities will only affect items reported above this line in the profit and loss account. The profit and loss account for The Equipment Manufacturing Company down to the operating profit level is shown in Figure 7.1.

Figure 7.1 Profit and loss account for The Equipment Manufacturing Company

		£k	£k
	Turnover		6,000
less	Cost of sales		4,000
	Gross profit		2,000
less	Distribution costs	100	
	Operating expenses	850	
			950
	Operating profit		1,050

It is important to understand the key items reported in the profit and loss account.

Turnover

The turnover represents the total amount of revenue earned during the year from the company's normal trading operations.

Cost of sales

This represents the direct costs of making the product that is sold. The costs are primarily labour and materials.

Gross profit

When the cost of sales is removed from the turnover, the resultant figure is the gross profit. This gives a direct comparison between what the product can be sold for and what it costs to make. This 'margin' has to be sufficient to cover all of the costs and overheads incurred in running the business.

Other costs

These would include distribution costs, administration and operating expenses. This includes the cost of running the sales and marketing department together with advertising and promotional costs. It would also include head office salaries, rates, electricity, depreciation and the cost of research and development.

Operating profit

This is the key figure in the accounts as far as we are concerned. It is the net result of trading for the year, when total sales revenue is compared with the expenses incurred in earning that revenue. It is the ultimate measure of whether it has been worthwhile staying in business.

Exercise

Before you start budgeting for your marketing plan you need to familiarize yourself with the accounting practices used within your own company or business unit. If you do not already have them, you should obtain copies of your company's profit and loss account and get your accounts department to explain how the distribution costs and operating expenses are calculated and allocated.

Budgeting the cost of a marketing plan

Your marketing plan is part of your company business plan. Individual marketing plans are ultimately collated into the overall company marketing plan. The principles are the same whether you are preparing the sales budget for the overall company marketing plan or calculating the effect of an individual marketing plan. However, in budgeting and evaluating individual marketing plans, we only need to consider part of the company budgeting process. This is shown in Figure 7.2.

Figure 7.2 Budgeting for additional sales

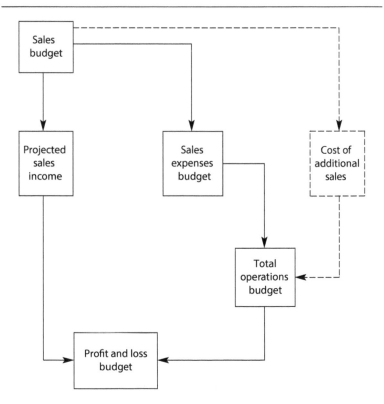

It is only if your product is a new one or if you are forecasting considerable increases in business from your plan that major capital investment may also be required. Obviously, if your plan includes an increase in field sales personnel, there will be additional requirements for company cars, laptops and mobile phones, which must be budgeted for.

With a marketing plan for an individual product or market, we are not considering the total company turnover and costs, but only the additional turnover generated by the plan and the costs associated with its implementation.

There are a number of techniques that allow you to predict whether the extra business that you will generate from your plan will be profitable or not. One of the simplest is to cost up all of the expenses that you intend to incur in implementing your plan and to compare these with the contribution that will be generated by the additional sales turnover that will result from your plan. For individual plans this method is quite adequate and we will use it here. (When a new product is being introduced more complex techniques such as break-even analysis or payback analysis can also be used. These techniques are explained further in my book *The Marketing Plan*, also published by Kogan Page.)

It is necessary to cost up all of the action plans for all of the different strategies through which you intend to achieve your objectives.

First let us look at the operating expenses budget for the UK sales department of The Equipment Manufacturing Company before the implementation of the marketing plan. This is shown in Table 7.1.

Table 7.1   Example of operating expenses budget

Operating expenses budget for 20X6 Department: UK Sales					
Item	20X5 expenses £k	Inflation %	£k	Growth £k	Other £k	20X6 £k
Salaries	160	3	4.8	75		239.8
Recruitment	3	3	0.1	6		9.1
Travel/entertaining	30	3	0.9	7		37.9
Car costs	14	3	0.4	6		20.4
Advertising	10	3	0.3	11		21.3
Exhibitions	10	3	0.3		28	38.3
Literature	10	3	0.3		5	15.3
Sundry items	10	3	0.3			10.3
Total	247	3	7.4	105	33	392.4

Now we will prepare a partial profit and loss account for The Equipment Manufacturing Company based on the *additional costs* of implementing the UK marketing plan.

In preparing this profit and loss account budget, we start at the top with the forecast sales. Here we are only showing the *additional sales*. The cost of sales is the direct cost, in materials and labour, of making the budgeted amount of product sold. The gross profit is the 'margin' to cover other costs and to contribute to profits.

In carrying out the marketing plan, the operating expenses incurred will relate to different departments. Most of the costs will relate to the sales and marketing department, but they will include administrative recharges for the management of company cars, allocation of office space (rent/rates/heating/lighting), and computer management and maintenance.

The costs incurred by the sales and marketing department represent the cost of extra items such as literature, advertising and exhibitions and the cost of salaries and travelling expenses related to the additional staff included in the plan. They will include the costs of the advertising campaign and exhibition for the water industry shown in Table 6.1 and Figure 6.4. The costs of the existing salesforce (shown in Table 7.1) are already included in the overall company profit and loss budget and do not therefore need to be included again in this partial profit and loss budget.

The partial profit and loss account for the additional sales included in the UK marketing plan is shown in Table 7.2.

Table 7.2 Effect on profit and loss account of additional operating expenses for implementing UK marketing plan

	20X6 £k	20X7 £k	20X8 £k
Invoiced sales	260.0	576.0	937.0
Cost of sales	158.6	339.8	534.1
Gross profit	101.4	236.2	402.9
Sales and marketing costs			
Salaries	75.0	78.0	81.1
Recruitment	6.0		
Travel/entertaining	7.0	7.6	7.9
Car costs	6.0	6.2	6.5
Advertising	11.0	11.5	12.0
Exhibitions	28.0		15.0
Literature	5.0	25.0	20.0
Sundry items		5.0	6.0
Total sales costs	138.0	133.3	148.5
Administration costs	20.0	20.8	21.6
Data processing costs	5.0	5.5	6.0
Distribution costs	6.9	7.2	7.5
Total operating expenses (relating to plan)	169.9	166.8	183.6
Operating profit (relating to plan)	(68.5)	69.4	219.3

It can be seen that the plan shows a loss in its first year and only breaks even in year two. This is quite normal. It would be nice if we could always plan to break even straight away, but in the real world it is often necessary to invest first and reap the rewards later. It would be of concern if break even was later than the second year because it would then become a vanishing horizon. In this case it would be wise to reconsider the plan.

Exercise

Now detail the initial operating expenses budget for the sales department in your plan. Also prepare a partial profit and loss account for the additional sales and additional costs included in your plan.

_____

_____

_____

_____

_____

_____

_____

_____

_____

_____

_____

_____

Summary points

Because there is no point in proceeding with a marketing plan unless it is going to increase company profits, you need to be able to evaluate its cost-effectiveness.

You need to:

- consider the additional turnover and contribution generated by the plan;

- consider and budget for the extra costs associated with its implementation;

- prepare a partial profit and loss budget;

- evaluate the cost effectiveness of the plan;

- confirm that the return in increased contribution and profit justifies the expenditure involved.

08
Writing the plan

Now that you have collected all of the information for your plan, you can prepare the written document and set about communicating it effectively to the relevant people in your company.

Top tip

The written plan should only contain the key information that needs to be communicated – it should be clear and concise, and excessive or irrelevant detail should be excluded.

The bulk of the internal and external market research information collected in the course of the preparation of the plan should not be included in the written plan since this would only confuse the reader. The detail of all of the individual action plans would also be excluded from the main document – although a summary of very important action plans may be included. Other key information that you want to include should be put in appendices and not in the main document.

The written plan must be clear, concise and easy to read. The following points give some guidelines:

- Standardize your headings. Put main section headings in bold to differentiate them.
- When listing key points, use double spacing and, where appropriate, use bullet points.
- Do not try to cram too many tables or graphics onto one page.

- Do not reduce the size of documents scanned into the plan to a point where they become difficult to read.

- Use a reasonably large font size when printing the document (12 pt or 14 pt).

- If the plan is too long it will just not be read, so be ruthless and cut out unnecessary text.

- Do not use jargon that may not be understood by all those who will receive the plan, and be sure to expand any abbreviations to their full form at their first appearance.

If you are careful in the way that you write the plan you can use many of the individual sections as presentation slides.

You should start with a table of contents which will enable the reader to quickly locate the various sections of the plan. Figure 8.1 shows how the table of contents should be set out.

Depending on the scope of your plan, you may need to omit or combine certain sections.

Figure 8.1 Contents list of a complete marketing plan

CONTENTS		
	Section	**Page**
1	INTRODUCTION	2
2	EXECUTIVE SUMMARY	3
3	SITUATION ANALYSIS	4
	– Assumptions	4
	– Sales (History/Budget)	5
	– Strategic Markets	7
	– Key Products	9
	– Key Sales Areas	11
4	MARKETING OBJECTIVES	13
5	MARKETING STRATEGIES	14
6	SCHEDULES	18
7	SALES PROMOTION	19
8	BUDGETS	20
9	PROFIT AND LOSS ACCOUNT	22
10	CONTROLS	23
11	UPDATE PROCEDURES	24
	APPENDIX 1	26
	APPENDIX 2	32

Introduction

This gives the background to the plan, and the reasons for its preparation, and outlines its purposes and uses.

The introduction to the UK plan for The Equipment Manufacturing Company is as follows:

UK sales have stagnated in recent years. The company has always sold a reasonable amount of product into the water industry, but it has never been a key activity area. Because of this, we knew little of the industry or of the potential in it for our product. With the enforcement of directives for water treatment and sewage disposal, the industry is now again carrying out a major capital improvement programme. It was therefore felt by the sales and marketing director that we needed to analyse our position in the market and prepare for growth to take advantage of the increased level of spending by the industry.

Exercise

Prepare an introduction for your plan:

_____

_____

_____

Executive summary

The summary should present the key points of the plan in a clear and concise form. It should not be too long or verbose. All personnel reading this plan should be able to understand the essence of the plan from this summary.

The summary should always include:

- the underlying assumptions on which the plan is based;
- the objectives of the plan;
- the timescale over which the plan will be implemented.

Although you can draft out an executive summary at any time, you cannot finalize the text until the plan is complete.

The executive summary of the UK marketing plan for The Equipment Manufacturing Company is given below:

Although our total sales in the UK market have fallen, sales of filters have tripled in the last three years. The increase in filter sales has been mainly into the water industry. Our problem area has been ball valves where we only have a 10 per cent market share, with low sales in the water industry. We currently have market shares in the water industry of 10 per cent for filters and 5 per cent for valves. We believe that if economic conditions remain stable, we will be able to gain market share in this expanding market. Also, the packaging of our filters and valves together will give us a competitive advantage.

The objective of this plan is to achieve 10 per cent growth in UK sales in real terms over the next three years, doubling our water industry market share for filters to 20 per cent and doubling our market share for ball valves to 10 per cent of the projected market in 20X8. In doing so, we intend to increase UK overall gross margins from 39 per cent to 43 per cent by 20X8. This plan details how this can be achieved with an investment in personnel and resources, but without any major additional investment in plant and machinery.

Exercise

Sketch out your first attempt at an executive summary for your plan. This should then be checked and, if necessary, amended when your plan is complete:

_____

_____

_____

Situation analysis

In the written plan, the situation analysis should include only the summaries of the external and internal marketing research and the key resulting SWOT analysis. These are included under the headings:

- assumptions;
- a summary of historical and budgeted sales;
- a review of strategic markets;
- a review of key products;
- a review of key sales areas.

There will be some overlap between the reviews of strategic markets, key products and key sales areas, because it is possible to show the mix in different ways. The important thing is to present the information in a manner that highlights the key points you are trying to convey to those who read the plan. Often the SWOT analyses are put together in the appendix.

Assumptions

These are the key facts and assumptions on which the plan is based. They should be few in number and should relate only to the key issues which would significantly affect the likelihood of the plan's marketing objectives being achieved.

Each assumption should be a brief factual statement. For example:

- The £/$ exchange rate will remain in the range $1.30 to $1.50:£1 for the next 12 months.

- Interest rates will not increase by more than 1 per cent over the next three years.

- Company wage increases will not exceed inflation over the next three years.

The Equipment Manufacturing Company has made the following assumptions with regard to its UK marketing plan:

- Inflation will remain at 3 per cent in 20X6, rising to 4 per cent in 20X7 and 20X8.

- Company wage increases will not exceed inflation over the next three years.

- The pound sterling will not strengthen against either the euro or the US$ during the timescale of the plan.

- There will be no delay in the timescale for the UK water industry to implement the directives on drinking water and effluent.

Exercise

List the assumptions that you will include in your marketing plan:

- _____

- _____

- _____

- _____

Sales

In this section you should include historical sales going back three years together with sales forecasts for the next three years. Unless you state otherwise, it will be assumed that the years shown in your forecast are calendar years. You should use invoiced sales rather than order intake figures as the basis of the plan, because other departments in the company, such as production and finance, can only operate on sales figures. You will, however, need to include order intake figures in your plan as well, because these will be the order budgets that the sales department will work to. More detail would normally be included with regard to the next 12 months' sales forecast since this will become the annual budget for the product or area covered by the plan.

In this section under *Sales* you would normally only include the sales projection for the total area and products. A more detailed breakdown into individual products and sub-areas would be included under key products, key sales areas or in the appendix to the plan. The format for setting out this information follows the guidelines given in Chapter 2.

The sales projection for The Equipment Manufacturing Company for the UK plan is shown in Table 8.1.

Exercise

Prepare a sales projection for your own company for your plan:

- _____
- _____
- _____
- _____

Table 8.1   Sales projection for the UK

The Equipment Manufacturing Company sales figures (historical and forecast)					
Sales area: UK					
	←——Actual——→			←—— Forecast ——→		
Year (all values in £k)	**20X3**	**20X4**	**20X5**	**20X6**	**20X7**	**20X8**
Filters	200	450	600	750	900	1,050
Valves	1,400	1,200	1,000	1,060	1,151	1,287
Components	300	350	400	450	525	600
Total	1,900	2,000	2,000	2,260	2,576	2,937

Strategic markets

In this section you should include historical information and forecasts for the company's sales in key industry sectors. The information can be presented in two ways:

1 showing the percentage of company sales into each market;

2 showing the percentage share of individual markets that the company believes that it has.

Only include your key markets – ideally this should be between three and six industries, because if you only sell to one industry you will be very vulnerable to changes or fluctuations within that industry.

This type of information can either be presented in tabular or graphical form. Tables 8.2 and 8.3 are representations for The Equipment Manufacturing Company in tabular form and Figure 8.2 in graphical form. You should also include some background notes on the key industries.

Table 8.2 Presentation of sales and market share by strategic market

UK sales – strategic markets				
Product: Ball valves	**Actual – 20X5**		**Forecast – 20X8**	
Industry	**£k**	**%**	**£k**	**%**
Chem/Petrochem	360	36	430	33
Water	150	15	300	23
Paper	120	12	150	12
Food	80	8	90	7
Other	290	29	317	25
Total	1,000	100	1,287	100

Table 8.3 Presentation of sales and market share by strategic market

UK sales – strategic markets				
Product: Filters and components	**Actual – 20X5**		**Forecast – 20X8**	
Industry	**£k**	**%**	**£k**	**%**
Chem/Petrochem	200	20	250	15
Water	400	40	900	55
Paper	150	15	220	13
Other	250	25	280	17
Total	1,000	100	1,650	100

Figure 8.2   Graphical representation of The Equipment Manufacturing
Company's strategic markets for ball valves

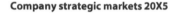

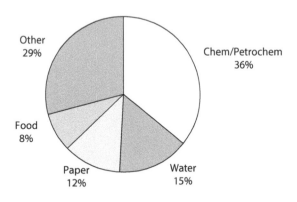

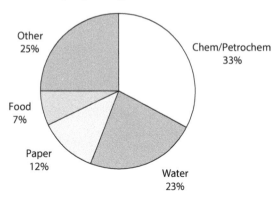

The narrative included by The Equipment Manufacturing Company
in their UK plan is as follows:

Chemical/Petrochemical industry
*The chemical/petrochemical industry is our biggest market
worldwide. In the UK it accounts for more than 25 per cent
of our total sales. Although it is a major source of revenue, the
market has been hit hard by the move in refining capacity and*

heavy chemicals production out of high-cost areas like Europe to the Far East and more recently to the US with its huge reserves of shale gas. We will do well to hold our own in this industry in the UK over the next few years.

Similar notes are included for other key industries.

Exercise

Prepare information on your strategic markets for inclusion in your marketing plan:

_____

_____

_____

Key products

This section lists your key products and details technological and commercial factors relating to them. This would include the results of the SWOT analysis on your products and your competitors' products. The information could be presented in a similar format to the data on strategic markets, or it could be included in a product portfolio matrix. A SWOT analysis for a product and the product portfolio matrix for The Equipment Manufacturing Company are shown in Figures 8.3 and 8.4.

The following narrative is included by The Equipment Manufacturing Company in their UK marketing plan:

Ball Valves
Our ball valve product is nearing the end of its useful life. We intend to carry out a customer/competitor survey over the next six months to define the market requirements for a new product. The development of the new product will take at least

18 months. In the meantime, we will continue to develop sales of the product as a component in our filter packages for the water industry.

Notes are also included on the company's ranges of filters.

Figure 8.3   SWOT analysis for product – ball valves

Strengths	Weaknesses
• Good range of sizes • Quality product • Solidly built	• Limited range of materials • Heavier than competitors' products • High cost/high price
Opportunities	**Threats**
• Source product from China • Develop new product	• Cheap imports from Asia • Competing products in plastic materials

Figure 8.4   Portfolio matrix of The Equipment Manufacturing Company

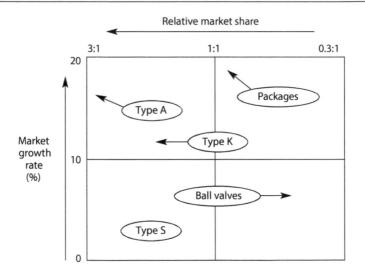

Exercise

Prepare key product information for the products included in your plan:

_____

_____

_____

Key sales areas

This information is presented in the same way as the information on strategic markets, but gives the information relating to geographical areas instead of industry sectors. The information can be presented in tabular form as in Table 8.4 or in graphical form as in Figure 8.5.

Table 8.4 Representation of key sales areas

The Equipment Manufacturing Company sales figures (historical and forecast)						
Sales area: UK Product: Ball valves	◄—Actual—►			◄—Forecast—►		
Year (all values in £k)	20X3	20X4	20X5	20X6	20X7	20X8
South	295	250	230	240	250	260
Midlands	485	415	360	370	390	420
North	525	420	300	325	351	422
Wales	45	55	60	65	70	75
Scotland/NI	50	60	50	70	90	110
Total	1,400	1,200	1,000	1,070	1,151	1,287

Figure 8.5 Graphical representation of key sales areas for ball valve sales for The Equipment Manufacturing Company

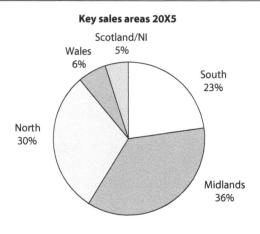

Key sales areas 20X5

Scotland/NI 5%
Wales 6%
South 23%
North 30%
Midlands 36%

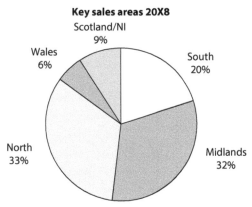

Key sales areas 20X8

Scotland/NI 9%
Wales 6%
South 20%
North 33%
Midlands 32%

In the narrative of your plan you should include relevant information on the size of each key market, growth rates, and your position in each market now and projected for the future. You should also include comments which may relate to your distributor, agent or other methods of distribution in that market.

Exercise

Prepare information on your own key sales areas:

_____

_____

_____

_____

_____

_____

Marketing objectives

This is a list of the objectives that are to be achieved, quantified in terms of order intake, sales turnover, market share and profit. In the written plan you should list your key objectives only. The key objectives are overall objectives.

The objectives included in the marketing plan for the UK for The Equipment Manufacturing Company are as follows:

• To increase UK sales by 10 per cent per year in real terms for the next three years.

• To double ball valve sales to the water industry within three years.

• To increase sales of packages to 50 units within three years.

• To double market share for filters in the water industry by 20X8.

• To double distributor sales in Scotland and NI by 20X8.

• To increase overall gross margins from 39 per cent to 43 per cent by 20X8.

Exercise

Now list the key objectives for your marketing plan:

_____

_____

_____

Marketing strategies

You should indicate whether you are adopting defensive, developing or attacking strategies – or a mixture of different types. The individual strategies should then be listed under the headings of the four main elements of the marketing mix:

- Strategies relating to products.
- Strategies relating to pricing.
- Strategies relating to advertising/promotion.
- Strategies relating to distribution.

There may be some overlap between the individual categories, but this does not matter so long as all of the strategies are listed.

In their plan, The Equipment Manufacturing Company are adopting a mixture of *developing* and *attacking* strategies.

Their key strategies are listed below:

Products

- Package products (ball valves with filters).
- Design new ball valve.
- Design replacement for 'type S' filters.

Pricing

- Additional discount will be offered for online purchases to encourage use of our online shop.
- Penetration policy will be adopted with packages since these will help us to sell more valves.
- Penetration policy will be adopted on 'type K' filters since these generate a large proportion of replacement cartridges.

Promotion

- Change salesforce organization.
- Recruit additional sales personnel.
- Restructure sales management.
- Increase advertising.
- Increase exhibition coverage.
- Use mailshots/e-mailshots.
- Add 'web analytics' for e-marketing.
- Update and expand website.

Distribution

- Change distribution.
- Appoint distributor sales manager.
- Increase own sales coverage.
- Expand online shop.

Exercise

Now list the key strategies for your marketing plan. Our key strategies are:

Products

_____

_____

_____

Price

_____

_____

_____

Promotion

_____

_____

_____

Distribution

_____

_____

_____

Schedule of what/where/how

This is the master schedule showing the programme for the implementation of the action plans. Each action plan would be listed either in the master schedule or in a sub-schedule for the functions of product, pricing, promotion or distribution. These schedules indicate to each department and to each member of staff their responsibilities and the timetable for carrying them out. They should take the form of bar charts. An example from the marketing plan of The Equipment Manufacturing Company is shown in Figure 8.6.

Figure 8.6 Master schedule for UK plan

Master schedule			
Area: UK Year: 20X6			
Month	**1 2 3 4 5 6 7 8 9 10 11 12**	**Responsibility**	
Action plan		Dept	Person
Restructure	————▶	Executive	RLT
E-mailshot	——▶	Marketing	AJK
Advertising	————————————▶	Marketing	AJK
Exhibitions	——————————▶	Marketing	AJK
Pricing	——————▶	Sales	EGM
Distribution	————————▶	Marketing	AJK
Market analysis	——————▶	Marketing	AJK
Product design	———————————▶	Engineering	TRG
Expand website	————————▶	IT	JAT

The detailed action plans would not be included in the main body of the marketing plan, but could be included in an appendix.

Exercise

Prepare a master schedule for your own plan:

_____

_____

_____

Sales promotion

Under this heading you should detail your advertising and promotions plan. This includes your personnel requirements as well as advertising and sales promotion.

You should define the mix of distribution channels that you will be using and the structure of your sales organization, including any changes that you intend to make as part of your plan. You should include a list of existing and additional sales personnel as well as an organization chart for the sales department. The charts can be included as an appendix to the main plan. Examples of the sales organization charts and the presentation of existing and additional personnel used by The Equipment Manufacturing Company in its plan were given in Chapter 6 in Figures 6.1, 6.2 and 6.3.

You should include the details and costs of your advertising and sales promotion campaigns. A detailed advertising and promotions schedule for the next 12 months should be included as an appendix.

Budgets and the profit and loss account

The minimum information that should be included is the total cost of implementing the plan. This needs to confirm that the return in increased contribution and profit justifies the expenditure in the action plans and the advertising and promotion plan. The budgeted extra costs will have an effect on the company profit and loss account. The additional sales projected by the plan and the extra costs involved must be presented in the written plan in a way that shows the extra contribution that the plan will make to company profits. The figures should be presented as shown in Table 7.2. They can also be presented as a complete profit and loss account for the area and products of the plan.

A complete profit and loss account for The Equipment Manufacturing Company for its UK sales operations with increased sales is shown in Table 8.5.

Table 8.5   Profit and loss account for UK operations

	20X6 £k	20X7 £k	20X8 £k
Invoiced sales	2,260	2,576	2,937
Cost of sales	1,356	1,507	1,674
Gross profit	904	1,069	1,263
Sales and marketing costs			
Salaries	239.8	249.4	259.4
Recruitment	9.1	3.2	3.4
Travel/entertaining	37.9	39.4	41.0
Car costs	20.4	21.2	22.0
Advertising	21.3	22.2	23.0
Exhibitions	38.3	11.0	26.4
Literature	15.3	36.0	31.7
Sundry items	10.3	10.7	11.1
Total sales costs	392.4	393.1	418.0
Administration costs	159.0	166.4	174.1
Data processing costs	32.0	33.3	34.6
Distribution costs	60.0	65.0	70.0
Total operating expenses	643.4	657.8	696.7
Operating profit	260.6	411.2	566.3

Exercise

Prepare a profit and loss account for your plan:

_____

_____

_____

_____

_____

_____

Controls and update procedures

Top tip

It is important to have a suitable monitoring and control system to measure performance in achieving the objectives of your marketing plan and to recommend corrective action where necessary. This monitoring and control system should be included in the written plan.

The control process involves:

- *Establishing standards* – these would relate to the budgeted sales and costs and the timescales for the implementation of the action plans.

- *Measuring performance* – this would compare actual performance against the standards.

- *Proposing measures to correct deviations from the standard* – by detailing corrective procedures to be implemented if the variation from standard exceeds certain limits. These limits should be defined in the written plan.

The control system will operate on the people who are responsible for implementing the plan rather than on the schedules and costs themselves. It should be easy to operate and should allow reasonable variations from the standards before it comes into action.

The controls should be detailed in the written plan. The Equipment Manufacturing Company has included the following controls in its plan:

There will be quarterly marketing plan meetings. A summary of costs against budget and actual progress against the schedules will be prepared for these meetings. A report on the implementation of the action plans will also be presented at these meetings.

Your marketing plan is not set in stone. As you implement it you will find that economic conditions may change, certain strategies may not be as effective as you thought and there may be delays in the implementation of some action plans. Conversely the plan may prove more successful than you anticipated and order intake levels expected in two years may be achieved in one year.

Because of this, an update procedure should be included in the written plan. This may simply state 'This plan is to be revised every 12 months'. Certainly all marketing plans should be updated on an annual basis.

Exercise

State the controls and update procedures for your plan:

_____

_____

_____

_____

_____

_____

Summary points

The written plan is the document that will transmit the detail of the plan to those who will implement it.

- The introduction should explain the background to the plan, the reasons for its preparation and its purposes and uses.

- The executive summary should present the key points in a clear and concise form.

- The information should be presented in a logical order.

- It should only include the key information that needs to be communicated.

- Excessive and irrelevant detail should be excluded.

09
Presenting the plan, follow-up and revision

You should now have completed your plan. You can compare it with the final version of the UK marketing plan for The Equipment Manufacturing Company which is shown at the end of this book.

Your task is not over when the written plan is complete. It must then be communicated – both to those who must agree to its implementation and to those who will implement it. If a plan is not properly communicated, it will fail. It will fail to be approved and it will fail in its implementation. So it is important to present the plan and to make sure that everyone understands it, rather than just sending a copy by email. If you have consulted properly during the preparation of the plan, it will be 'our plan' rather than 'my plan'. Remember that the contributors to the plan will be better motivated to help implement it if they have been involved in the planning process.

It can be a mistake to distribute the complete plan too widely – the UK sales manager does not need all of the detail of plans for export territories and likewise the export sales manager does not need all of the UK plan. A marketing plan is a sensitive and confidential document that would be of considerable interest to competitors and could be damaging in the wrong hands. Personnel do move on and they take information with them. Copies would obviously need to be supplied to senior executives of your company, but the plan should also be distributed to the heads of department such as accounts, R&D and manufacturing who would be affected by or involved in its implementation.

Presenting the plan

Presentation of the plan needs to be even more clear and concise than the written document itself. You may only have an hour – or even less – to present a plan that has taken many months to prepare.

Nowadays, everyone uses overhead presentations and I favour the use of the Microsoft Office software package with the Power-Point presentation programme. PowerPoint is not a difficult package to get to grips with, although becoming an expert requires training and lots of hard work. Almost anyone can start to use PowerPoint and prepare basic presentations with just a little guidance.

Simplicity is important in presentations and you want to make sure that when you make the presentation all present can easily read all of the slides. This means that you should use large font sizes and not try to cram too much writing onto one slide. If you are making the presentation before an audience, you should use a large screen and make sure that the projector is powerful enough for the presentation to be seen clearly.

You can also make your presentation to company members who are in other offices, other countries or working from home using a videoconferencing system. The use of computer-based video-conferencing systems expanded rapidly during the pandemic and the facilities available in the different programmes have also grown. The most popular programmes are Zoom and Microsoft Teams. The PowerPoint Live feature in Microsoft Teams allows you to start your PowerPoint presentation directly in a Microsoft Teams meeting without needing to share your screen with your audience. Accessing the 'chat window' directly alongside the presentation means that you shouldn't miss any important questions and it also allows the attendees to click on any hyperlinks and videos within the presentation at any point.

Top tips for preparing and making a presentation

- Use large font sizes for the text.
- Use an easy-to-read typeface such as Times New Roman or Arial.
- Don't try to get too many lines of text on a slide – about 10 is ideal.
- Use introductory slides with key headings and follow these up with separate slides expanding each of these headings.
- Bring bullet points in one by one to avoid the audience trying to read the whole slide rather than listening to your presentation.
- Consider using a background colour to enhance the impact of your presentation.
- Prepare a 'slide master' or 'background template' with your company name and logo on it.
- Include horizontal lines top and bottom to give your slides an 'active area'.
- Enhance your presentation by importing tables or graphs from Microsoft Excel (if applicable).
- Import suitable photos into your slides (if applicable).
- You can copy an open webpage onto a PowerPoint slide by pressing the 'Control (ctrl)' and 'Print Screen (PrtSc)' buttons together and then using the 'edit' and 'paste' functions in PowerPoint.

Figure 9.1 shows the PowerPoint template that The Equipment Manufacturing Company has prepared for use in its presentation. The letters 'EMC Ltd' and the seal at the bottom of the slide template are the company's housemark and corporate logo and are used on all company presentations. The heading 'Marketing Plan 20X6' is used just for this presentation.

Figure 9.1   PowerPoint template for use in marketing plan presentation

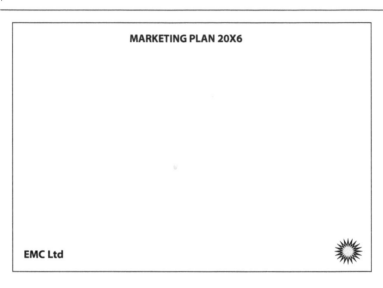

Figures 9.2–9.8 are some examples of a few of the PowerPoint slides that The Equipment Manufacturing Company has prepared for the presentation of its marketing plan.

Figure 9.2 Introduction slide

Figure 9.3 Sales areas

Figure 9.4   Valve sales by area

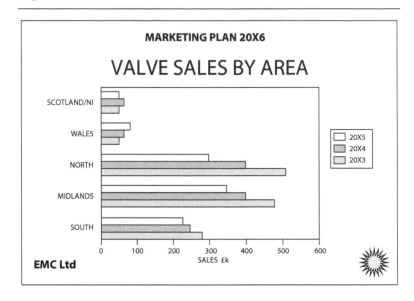

Figure 9.5   Objectives

MARKETING PLAN 20X6

KEY OBJECTIVES

- Increase UK sales by 10% per year
- Double ball valve sales to water industry
- Increase package sales to 50 per year
- Double filter market share in water industry
- Double distributor sales in Scotland/NI
- Increase gross margins from 39% to 43%

EMC Ltd

Figure 9.6 Strategic markets 20X8

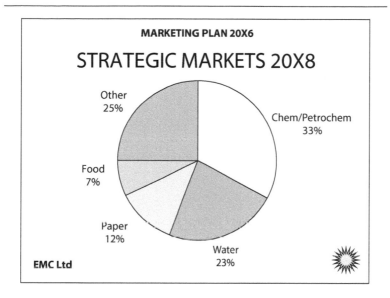

MARKETING PLAN 20X6

STRATEGIC MARKETS 20X8

Other 25%

Chem/Petrochem 33%

Food 7%

Paper 12%

Water 23%

EMC Ltd

Figure 9.7 Strategies

MARKETING PLAN 20X6

KEY STRATEGIES

Promotion

- Change salesforce organization
- Recruit additional sales personnel
- Restructure sales management
- Increase advertising
- Increase exhibition coverage
- Use mailshots/e-mailshots
- Update and expand website
- Add 'web analytics' for e-marketing

EMC Ltd

Figure 9.8   New sales structure

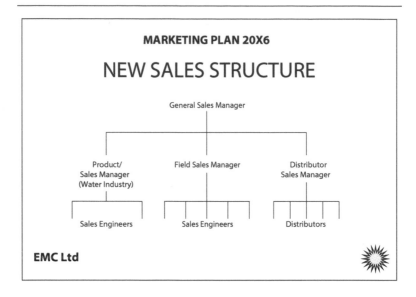

Follow-up and revision

Having written and presented your plan, now implement it, and you will start to see results. Your controls and update procedures will enable you to monitor progress and make changes.

Most companies use their marketing plans as a basis for the annual budgeting process. As you proceed with your plan, you can list the things that have gone well over the previous year and also the things that have gone badly. You should list your key tasks and give a status report on those that have been completed and those that have not.

And so the iterative process continues: from marketing plan to budget – from budget to update/revision of marketing plan – and on to the next budget. This iterative procedure can be simplified if you set up basic formats for both your marketing plans and budgets. The layout of the marketing plan that I have shown you in this book lends itself to being set up as a blank format in Word, with blank spreadsheets in Excel. If you lay it out with numbered pages, you can enforce a discipline with others in your company so that a common company standard is used for marketing plans and budgets and the presentation of both. This will also make it easier for those with less training or experience in marketing planning than you, to prepare the plans that are necessary for their part of the business.

The biggest advantage of a common format is that any individual plan can easily be incorporated into the overall company marketing plan, and sets of figures can be added together in interlinked spreadsheets.

Summary points

Presentation of the plan needs to be even more clear and concise than the written document itself.

- Simplicity is important.
- Use large font sizes.
- Don't cram too much writing onto one slide.
- Use a 'slide master' or 'background template'.
- Make face-to-face presentations.
- Bring bullet points in one by one.

10
Mini-plans and quick plans

In addition to preparing overall company marketing plans, there is often a need to produce small plans quickly for situations that arise and opportunities that present themselves.

Product plans

In Chapter 3 we considered methods of looking at and evaluating a company's product portfolio. The preparation of your product plan involves looking at your product portfolio and deciding:

- if it should be changed;
- how it should be changed;
- what strategies you can adopt;
- where these strategies will lead you.

But products and product portfolios are continually changing. Customers' requirements evolve and can also be influenced by developments and innovations coming from competitors. So companies will often need to react quickly and modify products, phase out old products, launch new replacement products and in some cases launch completely new supplementary products. Each of these product changes needs to be properly planned and a 'mini' or 'quick' plan can be prepared using the same outline structure as a full marketing plan. But whereas for a full company marketing plan, individual sections may be one or two pages long, in a mini-plan the same section may comprise just a few sentences or paragraphs. It would depend on the information that you have available and the summary information that you can put together quickly. But using the basic plan structure (as outlined in Figure 8.1) makes your plan look more professional and gives it credibility, even if it is based on a limited amount of information, research and analysis.

In the example marketing plan for The Equipment Manufacturing Company, they show a portfolio matrix for their range of products and say what they intend to do with their ranges of valves and filters. Their type 'K' cartridge filters and packages containing them are in a stage of rapid growth, while their type 'S' sand filters have reached saturation point. They intend to develop sales of their type 'K' cartridge filters/packages in the water industry and have prepared an individual mini-marketing plan for this product for their domestic market.

Our main business has always been selling valves to the water industry – a market that we know very well. We have also had some success in selling filter packages to water companies. Sales of filter packages with our type 'S' sand filters have fallen back, but last year we started selling packages with our new type 'K' cartridge filters and sales are now really starting to take off.

The Equipment Manufacturing Company
sales figures – projected sales of filter packages

Sales area: UK

Year (all values in £k)	Actual 20X3	Actual 20X4	Actual 20X5	Forecast 20X6	Forecast 20X7	Forecast 20X8
Filter packages (cartridge)			40	100	300	450
Filter packages (sand)	80	120	100	80	70	50
Total	80	120	140	180	370	500

Key Products

Many of our customers are not interested in building up units and would prefer to take filter packages. This will help us to sell our valves together with the filters

Packages with cartridge filters

We envisage that the bulk of the product we would offer would be cartridge filters. We would buy the cartridges from AMF Cuno and manufacture the housings ourselves.

Packages with sand filters

We would only supply small units (up to 1 cubic metre in size). We believe we could be competitive with these sizes of vessel.

Marketing objectives

- Grow sales of filter packages to £500k within three years.
- Grow sales of cartridge filter packages to £450k within three years.

Marketing Strategies

Product

- Offer cartridge filters and also small sand filters.
- Produce packages including these filters.

Pricing

- Offer discount structure to key contractors.

Promotion

- Mailshot/e-mailshot to water companies and water treatment contractors.
- Take part in Iwex exhibition at NEC in September 20X6.

Distribution

- Increase sales coverage by recruiting salesperson for the water industry.

Planning for a new product

When preparing a marketing plan for a completely new product, it is likely that there will be no historical data at all. Just because you do not have any historical data yourself does not mean that no useful data exists. There are many external sources that you can use. Even if there is no historical data relating to the new product, some market research would have been carried out to determine market size, competition, etc, and to estimate the potential market for the product. The methods used are the same as those used for making projections of the potential market for any product.

It is often the case that a product is superseding another product and in such cases historical data for that product should be used. Due note, however, should be taken of changes to the specification of the new product which may broaden its application.

There is also a difference in planning for a new product for a manufacturing company where they will probably be manufacturing the product themselves and for a small service company where the new product may be something bought in and just added to the range of products on offer.

Approaches for selected markets

Top tip

Just as basic marketing principles need to be adapted to the differences between consumer goods, industrial goods and services, consideration needs to be given also to regional and geographical differences.

In marketing planning it is important to consider the suitability of a product for a particular type of market.

Simple agricultural tools may find a ready market in developing and developed countries alike, but sophisticated capital equipment is more likely to find a market in developed countries. Even though luxury goods will be sold in developing countries, the size of the market for them will be proportionately larger in the richer industrialized countries or in developing countries with a large 'middle class' population.

So before considering selling into any new geographical market you should research that market and see how it fits in with your product, your capabilities and your existing markets.

Product

- Is your product suited to this market without changes?
- Will modifications be required?
- Will you need to expand your range?

Capabilities

- Are you well placed geographically to tackle this market?
- Do you have the resources, sales, admin and service?
- What will be the impact on your cash flow?

Market characteristics

- What are the market characteristics, size, customer base and customer type?
- How does this fit with markets you cover already?
- Will you need to train your staff in new techniques to tackle this market?

Marketing plans for individual export markets

> **Top tip**
>
> There is no fundamental difference between preparing a marketing plan for your domestic market and preparing plans for export markets.

As well as producing an overall export marketing plan, many companies involved in exporting need to produce more detailed operational marketing plans for individual countries. A useful illustration is given by the example below:

> The Equipment Manufacturing Company wants to grow sales in a number of export markets, but one market of particular interest is the US, which is already one of their biggest export markets. As part of their export plan, the export sales manager has prepared a sub-plan for the US market.
>
> *Our filter sales in the US market have grown over the last three years. This increase has been mainly into the water industry. We currently have market shares in the water industry of 10 per cent for filters and 5 per cent for valves. We believe that if economic conditions remain stable, we will be able to grow our filter sales in this expanding market. The packaging of our filters and valves together will give us a competitive advantage.*
>
> *The objective of this plan is to achieve 15 per cent annual growth in sales to the US in real terms over the next three years, doubling our water industry market share for filters to 20 per cent by 20X8 and maintaining our market share for ball valves at the same time.*

Assumptions

- US GDP will continue to grow at a rate of 2 per cent per year over the next three years.
- The pound sterling will not strengthen against the US$ during the timescale of the plan.
- Government policy with regard to grants for the construction of water and waste water treatment plants will remain unchanged over the next three years.

Sales (history/budget)

Sales area: US						
Year	←—— Actual ——→			←—— Forecast ——→		
(all values in £k)	20X3	20X4	20X5	20X6	20X7	20X8
Ball valves	500	550	450	500	525	550
Filters	200	290	400	475	550	650
Packages	85	185	300	410	520	600
Total	785	1,025	1,150	1,385	1,595	1,800

NOTE For consistency, all sales figures in this plan are given as net figures in £ sterling ex works our UK factory.

Key products

Ball valves

Our ball valve is an old style design and we are developing a new product which will be ready in about 18 months time. We will do well to maintain sales of individual valves at current levels but will develop sales of the product as a component in our filter packages for the water industry.

Filters

Sales of our 'type K' filters have doubled over the last three years. We expect this product to continue to grow.

Packages

Packages with our type 'K' cartridge filters are being specified in the water industry by contractors such as Black & Veach and Water Engineering. We expect sales to double over the next three years.

NOTE We sell virtually no replacement filter cartridges, because our distributors purchase these locally.

Strategic markets

Our strategic markets are chemicals/petrochemicals, water and paper. Sales in these markets to 20X5 and forecasts to 20X8 are given below:

Sales (history/budget)

Sales area: US Year (all values in £k)	← Actual →			← Forecast →		
	20X3	20X4	20X5	20X6	20X7	20X8
Chem/Petrochem	280	250	230	240	260	270
Water	100	350	460	650	820	990
Pulp and Paper	200	160	180	200	220	235
Other	205	265	280	295	295	305
Total	785	1,025	1,150	1,385	1,595	1,800

Chemical/Petrochemical industry

The chemical/petrochemical industry in the US accounts for 20 per cent of our total US sales. After decades of declining output, America's shale revolution has again turned the country into the world's biggest combined producer of oil and gas. This in turn has led to massive new investments in refining and petrochemical capacity. This has helped us to maintain our market share so far, but the increasingly strong local competition and the long-term move towards renewable energy and electric cars means that we will still do well to hold our own over the next few years.

Water industry

Sales in the water industry already account for 40 per cent of our US business. This is the fastest growing sector of our business. The industry is carrying out a major capital improvement programme to bring smaller water and waste water treatment facilities up to the levels required by the Clean Water Act. We expect to be able to take advantage of the increased level of spending in the industry.

Paper industry

The paper industry is slowly coming out of recession. Wood pulp prices have risen significantly in recent years and with the growth in the demand for coated paper we expect to see some increase in our valve and filter business. However, growth in the US market will be slow as new larger mills are being constructed in South America and Asia rather than at home.

Key sales areas

Sales of our ball valves have traditionally been in the North East, North Central and South Central United States, particularly in the chemical industry. The sales of our filters and packages are mainly aimed at the water industry, which covers the whole country. We are strong in the water industry in North East and North Central – particularly in New England, Pennsylvania and Illinois. We expect this rapid growth to continue now that we have signed up new agreements with water industry distributors for both our filters/filter packages and our valves.

Marketing objectives

- To increase US sales by 15 per cent per year in real terms over the next three years.

- To double sales of packages to 300 units a year within three years.
- To double market share for filters in the water industry by 20X8.

Marketing strategies

Products

- Package products (ball valves with filters).
- Design new ball valve (long term).

Pricing

- Increase discounts for packages to make it more attractive for distributors to sell these rather than individual filter units.

Promotion

- Produce US version of new brochure for filter packages and make files available to US distributors so that they can print them locally.
- Increase advertising targeted at the water industry in conjunction with key distributors.
- Take part in Chem Show in Cincinatti in June 20X6.
- Take part in Weftec Show in Chicago in October 20X6.

Distribution

- Evaluate and if necessary replace distribution in South East and on West Coast.

Sales promotion

We have good distribution through Chemical Services Company in Chicago, Water Services in Kenosha, Wisconsin and Petrochemical Services in Houston. We will evaluate our distribution in these areas and consider appointing these companies as 'master distributors/service centres'. Our sales in the South East and on the West Coast are minimal. The distributors in these areas should be evaluated and probably replaced.

Our main advertising expenditure will be targeted at the water industry. As well as taking part in The Chem Show each year as usual, we will take part in the Weftec Show (Water Environment Federation Technical Exhibition and Conference) in October 20X6.

Exercise

If you want to expand your export business or even if your company has no export business and you want to look into starting to export your products there is plenty of support available. Contact your local office of the Department of International Trade and arrange to discuss possibilities with your local International Trade Customer Support Coordinator. Contact details for regional offices are given on the website www.great.gov.uk.

Summary points

There is often a need to produce short plans quickly for situations that arise and opportunities that present themselves. Mini-plans are ideal where you need to:

- introduce a modified product;
- phase out an old product;
- introduce a new product;
- target a new sales area/individual sales area;
- develop sales in an individual export market.

APPENDIX

MARKETING PLAN
for
THE UK MARKET
20X6
THE EQUIPMENT MANUFACTURING COMPANY LTD
3 February 20X6

Contents

Section

8 Budgets and profit and loss account

9 Controls and update procedures

Appendices

1. Introduction

UK sales have stagnated in recent years. The company has always sold a reasonable amount of product into the water industry, but it has never been a key activity area. Because of this, we knew little of the industry or of the potential in it for our product. With the enforcement of directives for water treatment and sewage disposal, the industry is now again carrying out a major capital improvement programme. It was therefore felt by the sales and marketing director that we needed to analyse our position in the market and prepare for growth to take advantage of the increased level of spending by the industry.

2. Executive summary

Although our total sales in the UK market have fallen, sales of filters have tripled in the last three years. The increase in filter sales has been mainly into the water industry. Our problem area has been ball valves where we only have a 10 per cent market share, with low sales in the water industry. We currently have market shares in the water industry of 10 per cent for filters and 5 per cent for valves. We believe that if economic conditions remain stable, we will be able to gain market share in this expanding market. Also, the packaging of our filters and valves together will give us a competitive advantage.

The objective of this plan is to achieve 10 per cent growth in UK sales in real terms over the next three years, doubling our water industry market share for filters to 20 per cent and doubling our market share for ball valves to 10 per cent of the projected market in 20X8. In doing so, we intend to increase UK overall gross margins from 39 per cent to 43 per cent by 20X8. This plan details how this can be achieved with an investment in personnel and resources, but without any major additional investment in plant and machinery.

3. Situation analysis

3.1 Assumptions

- Inflation will remain at 3 per cent in 20X6, rising to 4 per cent in 20X7 and 20X8.

- Company wage increases will not exceed inflation over the next three years.

- The pound sterling will not strengthen against either the euro or US$ during the timescale of the plan.

- There will be no delay in the timescale for the UK water industry to implement the directives on drinking water and effluent.

3.2 Sales (history/budget)

Sales projection for the UK

The Equipment Manufacturing Company sales figures (historical and forecast)						
Sales area: UK	◄—— Actual ——►			◄—— Forecast ——►		
Year (all values in £k)	20X3	20X4	20X5	20X6	20X7	20X8
Filters	200	450	600	750	900	1,050
Valves	1,400	1,200	1,000	1,060	1,151	1,287
Components	300	350	400	450	525	600
Total	1,900	2,000	2,000	2,260	2,576	2,937

Refer to appendix 1.01–1.06 inclusive for details of sales and orders for the period 20X3 to 20X5 inclusive and for the sales and order budgets for 20X6 to 20X8 inclusive.

3.3 Strategic markets

Our strategic markets are chemicals/petrochemicals, water, paper and food. Sales in these markets for 20X5 and forecasts for 20X8 are given below:

Ball valves

UK sales – strategic markets				
Product: Ball valves	Actual – 20X5		Forecast – 20X8	
Industry	£k	%	£k	%
Chem/Petrochem	360	36	430	33
Water	150	15	300	23
Paper	120	12	150	12
Food	80	8	90	7
Other	290	29	317	25
Total	1,000	100	1,287	100

Filters and components

UK sales – strategic markets				
Product: Filters and components	Actual – 20X5		Forecast – 20X8	
Industry	£k	%	£k	%
Chem/Petrochem	200	20	250	15
Water	400	40	900	55
Paper	150	15	220	13
Other	250	25	280	17
Total	1,000	100	1,650	100

Chemical/petrochemical industry

The chemical/petrochemical industry is our biggest market worldwide. In the UK it accounts for more than 25 per cent of our total sales. Although it is a major source of revenue, the market has been hit hard by the move in refining capacity and heavy chemicals production out of high-cost areas like Europe to the Far East and more recently to the US with its huge reserves of shale gas. We will do well to hold our own in this industry in the UK over the next few years.

Water industry

Sales in the water industry already account for 28 per cent of our UK business. This is the fastest growing sector of our business. The industry is carrying out a major capital investment programme to comply with directives for water treatment and sewage disposal. We expect to be able to take advantage of the increased level of spending in the industry.

Paper industry

The paper industry is slowly coming out of recession. Wood pulp prices have risen significantly in recent years and with the growth in the demand for coated paper we expect to see some increase in our valve and filter business. However, growth in the UK market will be slow.

Food industry

Our sales into the food industry are declining. They currently only account for 6 per cent of our UK sales. Competition from stainless steel ball valve suppliers in the Far East is intense and increasing.

Strategic customers

From the 20X5 sales analysis, a list was produced of our major customers. This list (shown in appendix 3.01) contains our top 40 customers in terms of turnover and represents 20 per cent of the customer base and 80 per cent of total UK sales.

Because of the small customer base, ie only 806 accounts in 20X5 and a large amount of business coming from a small number of customers, it is important that our customer base is expanded and developed.

3.4 Key products

The portfolio matrix for our range of products is shown below.

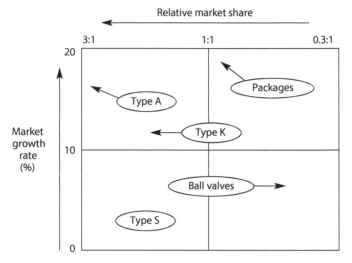

Ball valves

Our ball valve product is nearing the end of its useful life. We intend to carry out a customer/competitor survey over the next six months to define the market requirements for a new product. The development of the new product will take at least 18 months. In the meantime, we will continue to develop sales of the product as a component in our filter packages for the water industry.

Filters

The 'type S' filters have reached the 'saturation' stage of their life cycle, 'type A' filters are at the 'mature' stage of development and the 'type K' filters and packages are in a stage of rapid growth. We expect this to continue.

3.5 Key sales areas

The Equipment Manufacturing Company sales figures (historical and forecast)					
Sales area: UK **Product: Ball valves**					
	← Actual →			← Forecast →	
Year (all values in £k)	20X3	20X4	20X5	20X6	20X7	20X8
South	295	250	230	240	250	260
Midlands	485	415	360	370	390	420
North	525	420	300	325	351	422
Wales	45	55	60	65	70	75
Scotland/NI	50	60	50	70	90	110
Total	1,400	1,200	1,000	1,070	1,151	1,287

The Equipment Manufacturing Company sales figures (historical and forecast)					
Sales area: UK **Product: Filters and components**					
	← Actual →			← Forecast →	
Year (all values in £k)	20X3	20X4	20X5	20X6	20X7	20X8
South	120	252	350	445	565	655
Midlands	164	248	298	348	387	435
North	182	245	277	308	345	395
Wales	20	30	39	51	65	85
Scotland/NI	14	25	36	48	63	80
Total	500	800	1,000	1,200	1,425	1,650

Sales of our established products have traditionally been in the Midlands and the North of England, particularly in the chemical industry. The sales of our filters and components are mainly aimed at the water industry, which covers the whole country. We are particularly strong in the water industry in the south of England with Thames, Southern and Wessex Water. We expect this rapid growth to continue now that we have signed a framework agreement with Thames Water.

The valve business in the Midlands and the North of England has been particularly hard hit by the recession. We expect some improvement now with this product in these areas, but because of plant closures we will not reach the levels of sales that we have achieved in the past.

4. Marketing objectives

- To increase UK sales by10 per cent per year in real terms for the next three years.
- To double ball valve sales to the water industry within three years.
- To increase sales of packages to 50 units within three years.
- To double market share for filters in the water industry by 20X8.
- To double distributor sales in Scotland and NI by 20X8.
- To increase overall gross margins from 39 per cent to 43 per cent by 20X8.

5. Marketing strategies

Products

- Package products (ball valves with filters).
- Design new ball valve.
- Design replacement for 'type S' filters.

Pricing

- Additional discount will be offered for online purchases to encourage use of our online shop.
- Penetration policy will be adopted with packages since these will help us to sell more valves.
- Penetration policy will be adopted on 'type K' filters since these generate a large proportion of replacement cartridges.

Promotion

- Change salesforce organization.
- Recruit additional sales personnel.
- Restructure sales management.
- Increase advertising.
- Increase exhibition coverage.
- Use mailshots/e-mailshots.
- Update and expand website.
- Add 'web analytics' for e-marketing.

Distribution

- Change distribution.
- Appoint distributor sales manager.
- Increase own sales coverage.
- Expand online shop.

6. Schedules

Master schedule for UK plan:

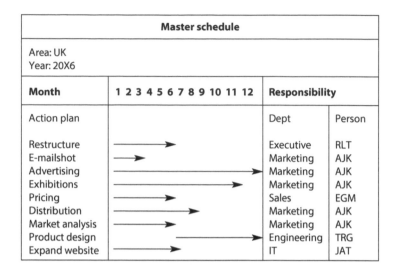

Master schedule		
Area: UK Year: 20X6		
Month	**1 2 3 4 5 6 7 8 9 10 11 12**	**Responsibility**
Action plan		Dept	Person
Restructure	——————►	Executive	RLT
E-mailshot	————►	Marketing	AJK
Advertising	——————————————►	Marketing	AJK
Exhibitions	————————————►	Marketing	AJK
Pricing	——————►	Sales	EGM
Distribution	————————►	Marketing	AJK
Market analysis	——————►	Marketing	AJK
Product design	—————————————►	Engineering	TRG
Expand website	——————►	IT	JAT

The master schedule shown above is for 20X6. Provisional schedules for 20X7 and 20X8 are included together with the individual action plans in appendices 6 and 7.

7. Sales promotion

Our sales of valves are concentrated in the Midlands and the North of England, where we have good distribution – particularly through Chemserv in Manchester. We will evaluate our distribution in this area and consider whether it is viable to purchase Chemserv as a sales/distribution centre for the north. Our sales in Wales, Scotland and Northern Ireland are minimal. The distributors in these areas should be evaluated and possibly replaced.

Our existing sales structure is shown below:

With this structure, the sales engineers are selling to large key accounts and contracting companies and the UK sales manager is running the salesforce and distribution. This structure lacks focus and we are proposing to change it to the structure shown below.

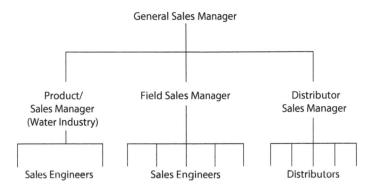

The present UK sales manager will become the field sales manager and we will promote the sales engineer who is our water industry expert to the position of water industry manager. We need to recruit three new people – a general sales manager, a distributor sales manager and a sales engineer.

Position	Existing personnel	New personnel	Total
General sales mgr		1	1
UK sales mgr	1		
Field sales mgr			1
Distributor sales mgr		1	1
Water industry mgr			1
Sales engineers	6	1	6
Total	7	3	10

Our main advertising expenditure will be targeted at the water industry. We will also continue our normal advertising/insertions in industry buyers' guides and yearbooks. We will carry out some targeted mail/e-mailshots and expand our website to include 'web analytics' for e-marketing. As well as taking part in The Pump and

Valve Exhibition each year as usual, we will take part in the International Water Exhibition in November 20X6 (this exhibition only takes place every three years). Our advertising schedule for 20X6 is shown below.

				Advertising											
Application: Water industry								Year: 20X6							
Media	No	Rate per insertion £	Total cost £	J	F	M	A	M	J	J	A	S	O	N	D
Water and Waste Treatment	2	1,800	3,600				X				X				
Water Services	2	1,500	3,000					X					X		
Water Bulletin	3	800	2,400			X			X			X			
Water products.com	1	2,000	2,000	X	X	X	X	X	X	X	X	X	X	X	X
Total cost			11,000												

8. Budgets and profit and loss account

Operating expenses for the UK operation will increase to fund the additional personnel and sales promotion costs of implementing this plan. The detailed operating expenses budget is shown below.

Operating expenses budget for 20X6 Department: UK sales					
Item	20X5 expenses £k	Inflation %	£k	Growth £k	Other £k	20X6 £k

Item	20X5 expenses £k	Inflation %	£k	Growth £k	Other £k	20X6 £k
Salaries	160	3	4.8	75.0		239.8
Recruitment	3	3	0.1	6.0		9.1
Travel/ entertaining	30	3	0.9	7.0		37.9
Car costs	14	3	0.4	6.0		20.4
Advertising	10	3	0.3	11.0		21.3
Exhibitions	10	3	0.3		28.0	38.3
Literature	10	3	0.3		5.0	15.3
Sundry items	10	3	0.3			10.3
Total	247	3	7.4	105.0	33.0	392.4

In subsequent years, we will not have such high exhibition costs and the recruitment costs will only occur in the first year. There will be increased costs for literature in years two and three when the new valve and filter products are launched.

The overall effect of the plan is to reduce profits in the first year. They will rapidly recover as our volume growth accelerates in the second and third years. The revised profit and loss account for our UK operations is shown below.

	20X6 £k	20X7 £k	20X8 £k
Invoiced sales	2,260	2,576	2,937
Cost of sales	1,356	1,507	1,674
Gross profit	904	1,069	1,263
Sales and Marketing costs			
Salaries	239.8	249.4	259.4
Recruitment	9.1	3.2	3.4
Travel/entertaining	37.9	39.4	41.0
Car costs	20.4	21.2	22.0
Advertising	21.3	22.2	23.0
Exhibitions	38.3	11.0	26.4
Literature	15.3	36.0	31.7
Sundry items	10.3	10.7	11.1
Total sales costs	392.4	393.1	418.0
Administration costs	159.0	166.4	174.1
Data processing costs	32.0	33.3	34.6
Distribution costs	60.0	65.0	70.0
Total operating expenses (relating to plan)	643.4	657.8	696.7
Operating profit	260.6	411.2	566.3

9. Controls and update procedures

There will be quarterly marketing plan meetings. A summary of costs against budget and actual progress against the schedules will be prepared for these meetings. A report on the implementation of the action plans will also be presented at these meetings.

This plan is to be revised every 12 months.

Appendices

I have not included all the appendices, but a list of them is shown below:

Appendix 1.01 to 1.06	Sales History and Budgets
Appendix 2.01 to 2.02	Unit Sales Analysis
Appendix 3.01	Major Customers
Appendix 4.01	Industry Sector Analysis
Appendix 5.01	Sales Territory Map
Appendix 6.01 to 6.02	Schedules
Appendix 7.01 to 7.08	Action Plans
Appendix 8.01 to 8.10	SWOT Analyses
Appendix 9.01 to 9.04	Competitor Analysis

Over 1.5 million
copies sold

All the books in the Creating Success series

Printed in the USA
CPSIA information can be obtained
at www.ICGtesting.com
JSHW072128020524
62407JS00016B/66